Life is an Adventure

Presented to

Rory MacLean

~~FREE CHURCH OF SCOTLAND~~
~~GLENURQUHART AND~~
~~FORT AUGUSTUS~~

Whoever trusts in the Lord, happy is he.
Proverbs 16:20

JUNE 2007

Life is an Adventure

Robert Murray McCheyne

Irene Howat

CHRISTIAN FOCUS

Copyright © 2004 Christian Focus Publications
ISBN 1-85792-947-0

Published in 2004
by
Christian Focus Publications
Geanies House, Fearn,
Ross-shire, IV20 1TW,
Great Britain

www.christianfocus.com
email: info@christianfocus.com
Thinking Further topics and timelines
Copyright © 2004 Christian Focus Publications

Cover design Alister Macinnes
Cover Illustration Neil Reed
Printed and bound in Great Britain by
Cox & Wyman, Reading.

Dedication

For Margaret and Jock

Contents

A Good Game of Squirrels 9

Winter Sets In 21

The Great Fire of Edinburgh.................. 31

David 41

Travels with Tully 53

Rescued from a Tree................................... 65

'Hey Minister!'... 77

Crash Landing!... 89

Journey of Discovery 101

An End and a New Beginning.............. 113

Thinking Further Topics 126

Timeline 132

Robert Murray McCheyne

Life Summary... 134

A Good Game of Squirrels

George saw his friend coming round the corner into the small village of Ruthwell. He dashed back into the garden to tell his brother.

'That's Robert now!' he yelled to Will. 'You go and hide in the den and we'll do things according to plan.'

Will raced round the back of the house and out of sight while George strolled through the garden and pretended to be surprised by Robert's arrival. When they met, they spun each other round till they both fell to the ground and couldn't get up again. Their heads were spinning. It took a couple of minutes for the world to settle down to where it should be and for the boys to untangle themselves from each other and get back on their feet.

'We've made a new den,' George said. 'But you've got to find it for yourself. The only clue is that it's in the garden. Count to a hundred, then come looking for us. Will's already there. Count loud so I know you're not cheating.'

George led his friend to the side of the house where Robert closed his eyes and began counting to a hundred at the top of his voice.

'One, two, three...' and George was off at a pelt to the left.

'Twenty-four, twenty-five, twenty-six...' said Robert, as his friend tiptoed behind him to the right.

'That'll confuse him,' George thought. 'I made plenty of noise going in the other direction so he's sure to think that's where I went.'

By the time Robert reached, 'Sixty-seven, sixty-eight, sixty-nine …' George had pelted through the vegetable garden, run along the blackcurrant bushes, and crawled behind an old door that was leaning against the high garden wall.

'He'll never find us here,' Will giggled when his brother reached him. 'But it'll be fun watching him try.'

'Ninety-eight, ninety-nine, a hundred!' shouted Robert McCheyne, before spinning round on his heels and surveying the scene behind him.

'He went this way,' Robert said to himself as he turned to his left. 'And he made a suspicious amount of noise about it. Still, I'll go have a look-see. And I'll be quiet about it.'

The boy walked silently on the grass till he reached the front of the house, then he backed against the wall and eased himself towards the front door. Just before he reached the door it opened and Mr Duncan came out. Thinking his cover was blown, Robert was about to say hello. But Mr Duncan had been a boy once himself, and he recognised the signs of a secret. Winking a welcome to the lad, he strode off down the path and out the gate.

'Someone will be pleased to see Mr Duncan coming,' thought Robert. 'I think everyone in Ruthwell likes their minister. My aunt certainly does.'

Passing the front door, Robert continued along the wall. As he went he looked for all possible cover, but he could see none at all. There were various places where they'd had dens in the past, but all were far too small to house two teenage boys and leave space for a visitor.

'I think George was being clever,' he decided, and he turned and went in the opposite direction. The den's more likely to be round the back anyway.'

Silent as a cat Robert retraced his steps. When he reached the corner of the house, he dodged behind a large rhododendron and took a run and jump for the garden wall, reaching the top in one.

'This will confuse the pair of them,' he thought. 'They'll be looking at ground level for me.'

Gently Robert eased himself along the wall, carefully avoiding decapitating himself on low-hanging branches! When he arrived at a point from which he was quite invisible from the back garden, he stopped and looked around.

'They could be behind the shed,' Robert thought. 'But that would be a bit tame. Then there's the shrubbery. There are plenty of hiding-places there. Hmmm.' The boy considered his options. 'There's always a possibility they've built something behind the wall of the compost heap.' He shook his head. 'But I think they've been cleverer than that.'

The old door caught his eye. 'One of them could hide behind there, but not both. In any case, an old door leaning against the wall isn't much of a den.'

In the absence of an alternative he pulled himself along the wall, keeping low and as far out of sight as possible. As he reached the door, he realised that it wasn't quite leaning against the wall. It had been wedged under a branch. The bottom of the door was a metre from the wall and the top was about half of that. When he peered into the darkness behind it the Duncan brothers were nowhere to be seen, but just then his eye caught something interesting. 'There's a rope hanging down behind the door,' he told himself. 'Very suspicious.'

The rope, he saw, hung down to ground level. Following the line of it upwards, he found himself suddenly eye to eye with Will Duncan, who was several branches above him.

'How on earth did you guess where we were?' laughed Will.

George was quick to chip in. 'I thought I'd given you the slip by making such a din when I went in the wrong direction.'

'That was a little too obvious,' grinned Robert. 'If you're thinking of becoming a professional burglar, think again. You'd spend all your life in prison.'

Robert grabbed the rope and used it to steady himself as he climbed up the branches to the wooden platform his friends had constructed in the beech tree.

'What do you think of it?' asked Will.

The visitor looked round. 'It's the best den we've had so far,' he said. 'But I'm afraid I found you quite by accident.'

George laughed aloud. 'Robert McCheyne, you just can't tell a lie! You can't even pretend to have worked out where we were!'

'But I didn't.'

Will and his brother looked at each other and winked. A year might have gone by since their friend last visited Ruthwell, but he was still the same decent and honest Robert Murray McCheyne. Not only that, they could tell from the mischief in his eyes that he was as much fun as ever.

'Squirrels?' said Robert.

His friends grinned.

'Squirrels it is!' they said together. 'And the first one round the garden and back to the den gets to choose what we do tomorrow.'

The three lads crawled along the branches, swinging from tree to tree as they went. The minister's garden had a high wall all round it, and the previous year the boys had discovered that they could circle the entire garden without touching the ground once. Will and George had practised over and over again and had worked out what they thought was the quickest route.

'Watch your head!' a voice called from above.

George Duncan looked up. Robert was two branches above him… and travelling fast! The den was within sight, and the race was tight.

'Go for it!' yelled Will from behind, though he wasn't sure which boy he was supporting!

Robert grabbed a branch of the beech tree, swung as far as he could and dropped to the wooden platform. But just a second earlier George had scrambled on and won the right to choose tomorrow's game. It took Will a little while to reach them as his trouser leg had caught on a branch. It seemed better to him to lose the race he was losing anyway than to risk an embarrassing darn on his trousers and a ticking-off from his mother.

Although George and Will were older than Robert, they looked forward to his visits to Dumfriesshire. George wondered if he had outgrown the kind of games they played, but it only took the world 'squirrels' to show that he was still a boy at heart. And he was glad about that.

'Are you three coming down for tea?' a voice asked from underneath the platform. It was Barbara, the third member of the Duncan family.

Robert was down in an instant to see his friend once again. But although Barbara's invitation was tempting he knew that his aunt was expecting him back.

'See you tomorrow,' he said. 'And you be thinking up something interesting for us to do, George!'

Setting out at a gallop, Robert left the village of Ruthwell and ran the short distance to Clarencefield. Not in the least out of breath he did a quick turn into Clarence Cottage and arrived at the door just as his aunt was taking scones from the flat iron girdle.

'I thought these would bring you home,' she said. 'Scones are like magnets to all the boys I know!'

The table was laid with oatcakes, butter, crowdie, scones and damson jam. Robert looked at it and grinned.

'You made every single thing yourself,' he laughed. 'These are home-made oatcakes and scones. You made butter from the milk from Maud, Mabel, Daisy and Ellen.'

Aunt Dickson smiled. She was pleased that her nephew remembered the names of her four milking cows.

'You strained the milk to make your own crowdie cheese too,' said Robert, licking his lips. 'And your damson jam is famous throughout the whole of Clarencefield.'

'Which would not be hard,' his aunt laughed aloud, 'seeing as there are just a handful of houses here!'

There was near silence for the next quarter of an hour as the boy savoured the warm welcome and the wholesome food. His aunt was quiet too. She was enjoying watching Robert eat every bit as much as he was enjoying eating. The only noise was the whistling of a yellow canary in his cane cage. When they'd finished tea, Aunt Dickson and Robert moved out into the glow of the late afternoon sun.

'Have you still got Geggely?' the boy asked, watching eight hens pecking in the garden.

'She's over there,' his aunt said. 'Behind the bushes.'

Right on cue a brown hen pecked her way round the bush and into full view.

'She lays the best eggs I've ever tasted,' commented Robert. 'Is she on the lay just now?'

His aunt assured him that Geggely would provide him with an egg each day.

'And the pigs?' he asked.

'Still there,' Aunt Dickson grinned, 'and still rooting around the orchard. They're counting the days until the first windfall apples land at their feet.'

'I counted the days until I finished school and came down here,' Robert said. 'I always do.'

Aunt Dickson looked at her nephew proudly. 'You did well at school, I'm told. And you won some prizes.'

Was it a blush or had Robert had a little too much of the sun? Either way, he was unusually red.

'Tell me what you enjoy doing at the High School in Edinburgh.'

Robert didn't have to think how to answer that question.

'I love Latin and Greek,' he said. 'And the best thing about learning ancient languages is that you can read books that were written hundreds and hundreds of years ago. They're full of exciting adventures and terrific battles. You should read them!'

Aunt Dickson laughed. 'Perhaps I've left it rather late to learn Latin and Greek.'

Grinning, Robert told his aunt when he had begun to learn Greek. 'I was four years old,' he said, 'and in bed ill, when the family taught me the Greek alphabet. It was something I could do without getting out of bed. I loved the sounds of the letters and the shapes of them on the paper. I think I've been interested in Greek ever since then.'

'Well it was worth being ill, wasn't it?' his aunt laughed.

Robert looked around him and smiled.

'I love coming to Clarencefield,' he said. 'This place feels just as much home as Edinburgh does.'

'And so it should,' Aunt Dickson said. 'Your father was brought up at Thornhill, which is only 20 miles from here. And your mother and I are from just up the road at Nether Locharwood. So of course you're at home here. You belong to these parts.'

The boy laughed. 'And I belong to Ruthwell because I got such a welcome from the Duncans that I couldn't help feeling at home there too.'

He had his aunt in stitches as he told her what they'd got up to that afternoon. She laughed aloud at Mr Duncan just walking past with a wink. 'He's so good-natured. All the young folk like their minister,' Aunt Dickson said. 'The poor people are very grateful to him, and not only in these parts.'

'Why grateful?' Robert wondered.

'Not long ago banks were only for wealthy folk. Poor people, even if they did manage to save a little money, could never open an account. They weren't welcome. Mr Duncan knew that, so he started the Savings Bank for poorer people to use. They can put just a few pence in at a time and save for what they need or for emergencies. One day there may be savings banks all over the country, and a good thing too.'

Robert was impressed by Mr Duncan's Savings Bank. 'Children could save in a bank like that,' he said.

His aunt nodded. 'Indeed they could. But it's time you did the rounds to see what these fine hens have to offer today. You'll find the nests in the barn as usual.'

Collecting eggs was one of Robert's favourite jobs. He took the basket and lined it with dry grass before going in search of Geggely. The afternoon was so warm that she was sound asleep on her nest and didn't look as though she wanted to be disturbed.

'Are you hiding an egg?' the boy asked, as he lifted the hen in such a way as to prevent her flapping her wings. Geggely opened a jet-black eye and peered at Robert. The beginnings of a protest began deep in her throat, but before she could gather an irritated cluck together Robert had her egg in his hand and she was back on her nest. Opening both eyes in surprise at finding herself where she wanted to be, the hen fluttered into a comfortable position and went back to sleep. When he had collected four eggs, he covered them with dry grass before looking for the others.

'Six laid today,' he told his aunt, as he went into the kitchen.

That night he wrote home to tell about his journey, his welcome at Clarencefield, the den at the manse, and to reassure his brothers and sister that Geggely was still alive and laying.

The summer was warm and dry, and before many weeks had passed the corn was golden and ready for harvest.

'Do you think I'm big enough to help make the stooks this year?' Robert asked.

Aunt Dickson eyed him up and down. 'I think you might be,' she said. 'Ask the Duncan boys to show you how.'

Robert was off like a shot to the manse. 'George!' he shouted, as he reached the gate.

His friend looked up from the potato patch.

'Wanting to help pick early potatoes?' he asked, forking a shaw[1] out of the earth. The lad sank to his knees and teased the roots apart before picking the little potatoes off the shaw. Then he gathered the larger ones that had fallen to the ground.

'Take some home with you for your dinner and have them with butter and greentails[2].'

---

[1] The plant/roots that potatoes grow from. [2] Chives.

'What are greentails?' Robert puzzled.

'Being a fine city gent you probably call them chives.'

Robert suddenly remembered what he had come for.

'Will you show me how to make stooks?' he asked.

George grinned. 'I thought you were big enough to do a man's job. Yes, I'll teach you, but I promise that it's a scratchy and itchy job.'

Feeling twice his height, Robert ran all the way back to Clarencefield to tell his aunt that he would help with the harvest after all.

'Lesson one,' George Duncan said the following day, when he and Robert met at the edge of the cornfield. 'You gather a sheaf of corn in your arms and lay it down on the ground. Then you pull a dozen or so stalks out of the sheaf and use them to tie the bundle together just under the heads of corn.'

Robert picked up an armful of corn and pulled a few stalks separate from it. Then he wound them round the bundle ... and stopped. 'How do you tie it?' he asked. 'The stalks break when I try to make a knot.'

His friend smiled. 'You don't make a knot at all. You wind the stalks round, twist them together, then tuck the ends in.'

It took a bit of doing, but eventually Robert managed to make decent sheaves. Then the second lesson began.

'You take two sheaves,' George said. 'And you lean them against each other like an Indian tepee. After that you lean a couple of sheaves on one side of the first two, and a couple on the other to make a stook. That lets the wind blow through between them to dry the corn.'

By the end of the day Robert knew what his friend had meant. After hours helping with the harvest he was happily tired, scratched and itchy as could be.

'It's the bath for you,' Aunt Dickson said, as she poured a pan of water into a tin bath on the kitchen floor. 'You deserve it!'

And so the summer of 1823 passed. Days were full of games with the Duncan boys, and sometimes with Barbara too, and with helping Aunt Dickson look after her pigs, hens and cows. He helped when the stooks were gathered into rickles, each of half a dozen stooks. And he watched when the rickles were forked into stacks. Fascinated, Robert watched the men thatch each stack with long strands of last year's corn so that the rain slid off rather than soaking in. When the time came to go back to Edinburgh, Robert felt he'd lived in the country all of his life.

'You've enjoyed yourself so much,' his aunt said, 'that you'll just have to come back again next year.'

'Try to stop me!' Robert laughed. 'Remember, you told me I belong here!'

Winter Sets In

Robert opened his eyes and jumped out of bed. He smiled as he stretched, for he had been dreaming about his summer holiday in Clarencefield. But when he pulled back his curtains he discovered that Edinburgh in January 1824 could not be more different from Clarencefield the previous summer. There was no bright summer sun, no warmth in the air, and … was that a snowflake falling or was it ash from an early-morning fire? Rubbing his eyes, the boy looked for signs of a snowy Saturday, but it was still dark outside.

Wrapping himself in his woollen dressing-gown, Robert lit a candle and picked up the book he has been reading before falling asleep. The candle guttered for a moment or two before settling down.

'The Last Days of Hercules,' Robert said to himself, 'It's a great story. Now, where did I get to?' he wondered, turning over the pages. 'I'd read about Hercules killing Iphitus in a fit of madness and going off for a year to serve as a slave for punishment.'

He knew the story so well that it was hard remembering where he'd got to this time round!

'Here we are!' he said, as he began to read. Robert was instantly transported back to ancient Greece. In his mind's eye he saw Deianira, Hercules' wife, waiting for her husband to return when a messenger arrived to say that he would soon be home, and bringing a gift from him. Robert imagined her sending a gift, a special charmed robe she had made, back to Hercules. But Deianira realised that the charm could kill her husband. Robert's eyes raced down the pages, so exciting did he find the story. When Deianira discovered that Hercules had been terribly wounded by the robe, she killed herself, and her husband died shortly afterwards.

Snapping the book shut, Robert realised it was daylight. He'd been reading for ages!

'I wonder if that was a snowflake,' he thought, as he tightened his dressing-gown and went to the window.

From his home in Edinburgh's Queen Street, Robert looked over the road to the neatly-kept gardens the residents of the street enjoyed. Beyond the gardens the land sloped downwards, and he looked over the trees and roof tops to the Firth of Forth in the distance. And beyond the grey wintry waters of the Forth he could see the hills of Fife. The Lomond Hills were not high, but they were high enough to be indicators of the weather in the middle of winter.

'There's snow on the Lomond Hills,' Robert said, 'and it's coming in this direction!'

He watched as the north wind blew snow-clouds over the Firth of Forth and grinned when the snowflakes started falling on Edinburgh.

'Wait till I tell David!'

Robert washed and dressed quickly before running downstairs to tell the family that it was snowing only to find that they were all in the dining-room already!

'Which of your Greek heroes kept you late for breakfast?' his father asked.

If Robert was ever late for anything it was because he had his nose in a book. Grinning, Robert explained that Hercules had held him back, but that there would be no holding him back now as it was snowing.

'I wondered when you'd notice,' laughed David. 'Snow on a Saturday… what could be better!'

By the time breakfast was over the snow was falling thick and fast.

'Fancy a walk in the gardens?' David asked his brothers and sister.

Eliza, Willie and Robert didn't need to be asked twice. The boys dressed in winter coats and their sister wrapped herself in a hooded cloak to keep out the worst of the north wind, then the four young people crossed Queen Street and went into the gardens.

'It's really heavy,' Robert laughed. 'We could run right round the gardens and see if we can get back to the gate before the snow covers our footprints.'

'I think it would be better if we walked quickly rather than ran because it was very hard frost last night and we don't want any broken bones,' advised Willie.

David winked. 'You can tell who's going to be a doctor!'

They set off at a cracking pace, making sure they made as clear footprints as they could.

'Why do you like the Greek myths so much?' Eliza asked her young brother.

Robert thought before answering. 'They're exciting,' he said. 'And you can learn a lot from them.'

'What about?'

'They're full of stories of courage and daring, and friendship and loyalty,' went on Robert. Then, noticing that his sister's hair had turned white in the heavy snow, he suggested that she tie her cloak tighter and put up the hood.

David laughed loudly.

'What's so funny?' Eliza asked.

David explained that Hercules was killed by a poisoned robe, and that she should watch out!

The four walked quickly round the perimeter of the garden, arriving back at the gate just as their first footprints disappeared under the heavy snow.

'Do you think we could build a snowman?' David asked, looking at the white blanket all around them.

Willie shook his head. 'Fine snow is better for that,' he explained. 'It holds together well.'

Seeing the disappointment in his young brother's face, Willie added that this snow was best for snowballs. The word was hardly out of his mouth when one hit him on the chest and Robert burst out laughing.

'Did you throw that, David?' Willie asked, and took his brother's laughter for a yes.

Within minutes snowballs were flying this way and that, and other young people emerged out of nowhere to join the McCheynes in their fun. But when David, Willie, Eliza and Robert crossed the road and went into number 56 they were wet beyond words. Eliza's hood had fallen down and a snowball caught in it had melted into a pool of water. The snow had gone over the top of Robert's boots and his feet were soaking wet. The two older boys brushed themselves down and sat by the fire to dry out, but Mrs McCheyne took charge of Eliza and Robert and they both ended up changing every single thing they had on.

'Now,' said Mr McCheyne, on 27th January, 'I think we should sit together round the fire for a while.'

The four young people grinned at each other. It was

their father's birthday, and that always involved some fun and games. But before that there was something just a little more serious.

'I'd like to read your birthday poem,' David told his father, when they were gathered around the fire.

Mr McCheyne smiled. He loved this tradition his middle son had started, of writing a poem for each of his parent's birthdays. Sitting back in his chair he listened as David read. The words of the poem were both serious and fun, thanking their father for being loving and kind.

'I'd like to tell you a poem too,' Robert said, 'but not a special birthday one.'

The boy launched into some verses he'd written about Hercules and Deianira, re-telling the story of the poisoned robe.

'I wondered if Robert was trying to poison me the day we had our snowball fight,' laughed Eliza, 'for he kept telling me to pull my robe tight about me.'

Story after story was told until Mr McCheyne said that it was now time for him to do some work in his study.

'But, Dad ...' Robert began.

Mr McCheyne looked in his youngest son's direction, and nothing more was said.

'He's a good lad,' thought the lawyer, as he closed the door behind him. 'I can't remember when I needed to do more than look at Robert for him to accept my word and stop arguing.'

'Are we ready for church?' Mrs McCheyne asked, the following morning.

She looked round the family and felt proud of them all. They looked fine in their Sunday clothes and with their Bibles under their arms.

'Let's go,' said Mr McCheyne. 'It's a long walk and the

pavements might be slippery.'

They were! And although some of the times Robert slid were accidental, others certainly were not.

The family walked all the way to the Tron Church for the morning service, and because it was too far to walk twice on an icy day they stayed there until the afternoon service was over. In between the services the young people filed into the church seats for questions and answers. One of the elders read questions from the Catechism and the children answered in turn. They practised psalm-singing too.

'It's amazing how quickly the time passes between the services,' David said, as they walked back home in the late afternoon.

Robert looked at his favourite brother. 'David loves going to church,' he thought. 'I like it too, but somehow it's really special to him.'

When Monday morning dawned Robert was up first as usual. He enjoyed school and looked forward to the new week. Dressing himself in his school clothes - including green tartan trousers - he got himself organised for the day ahead. As dawn broke he looked around his comfortable room and his mind wandered to Edinburgh's Cowgate, where some of the other High School pupils lived. Taking his pencil and sketch pad Robert drew part of the Cowgate from memory. He drew a narrow winding alleyway with tall buildings on either side. The upper parts of the buildings were higgledy-piggledy and even closer together than those at street level, until people leaning out of the top floor windows could nearly shake hands with those living on the other side of the street!

'If the buildings were two storeys higher they would

join together at the top and make the Cowgate into a tunnel,' laughed Robert.

With his pencil held on the slant he shaded the picture until it was very dark, then he drew the cobbled-stoned street.

'I'll have to make it dark at street level,' Robert thought as he drew. 'Very little sunlight gets down that far.'

Putting the drawing on the mantelpiece, the boy looked at it from a distance. Then he took it down again and began to sketch in some people. By the time he had finished, his drawing of the Cowgate looked very full and busy. Women stood in doorways talking to each other. Men trundled carts of goods for sale and children played hide-and-seek in and out of the bends on the alleyway. A few clever areas of shading showed that the children were not very clean, and gave the whole drawing a sad and rundown look.

'The Cowgate couldn't be more different from Queen Street,' thought Robert, as he looked around his room. 'I don't know how the High School boys who live there ever get peace and quiet to study.'

Being winter, it was growing dark as Robert set off home from school with two friends from Queen Street. Although it was quite a long walk they weren't in any great hurry. As they came out of the High School in Infirmary Street and turned on to the South Bridge, lights began to shine in some of the tall buildings around them.

'I remember coming along here with David and Willie one night before I went to school,' Robert told his friends. 'Gaslight had just been put in the buildings in the South Bridge and they brought me over to show me them. I was so excited!'

Robert laughed. 'When I was little I used to think it

was scary having streets of houses below long bridges! I once told Dad that I'd never walk under the Bridges in my life in case they fell down on top of me.'

'And have you?' his friend asked.

Laughing heartily, Robert admitted that he had... and he'd survived the experience!

'What did you do at school today?' Willie asked his young brother at dinner-time.

'We had Greek first and I read a verse I'd written in Greek.'

Willie raised his eyebrows in appreciation.

'Then we had history and in the afternoon we did maths.'

'Let me guess,' teased Willie. 'You enjoyed the morning better?'

Robert grinned. He could do maths fine, but he loved Greek and he loved poetry too.

'Have you homework to do?' his older brother asked.

'Just reading,' was the reply. 'But for next week I've to find out about the building of the Mound.'

'I'll help you with that on Saturday, if you like,' Willie volunteered, '... if you'll help me with what I've got to do.'

Looking puzzled, Robert asked what he could teach a medical student.

'We're studying feet and ankles in anatomy. I'd like to have a look at yours and to draw them too.'

'Easy-peasy homework,' laughed Robert, who loved drawing.

After dinner the lad sat back on a couch with his feet on a stool. While Willie drew his feet from several different angles, Robert drew his brother's face and profile. He was good at that, and made quite a collection of family drawings. Then because Willie was still busy, the lad drew a self-portrait from his reflection in the mirror.

'Do you think I could be a doctor when I'm older?' Robert asked.

Willie, who was struggling to draw his brother's big toe, didn't look up when he answered.

'No, I don't think you'll be a doctor. I think you'll study Latin and Greek and end up teaching at Edinburgh High School.'

The younger boy thought for a minute.

'I wouldn't mind that,' he said. 'Then I'd be able to read all the books I want to read. And I could go to Greece and Rome to see the ancient places…and I could draw them all and bring them home to show you.'

'But I might be away from home by then,' commented Willie.

Suddenly very interested in his brother's plans, Robert asked where he was thinking of going.

'I'm not sure,' was the hesitant answer. 'But doctors are needed everywhere. I could even go as far away as India.'

'If you go to India I'll save up and come to see you.'

Having finished his drawing, Willie tickled Robert's feet and suggested that he start saving right away.

One of Robert McCheyne's school friends joined the Saturday exploration of the Mound. Willie, who was good at explaining things, never stopped talking!

'When our house, and all the others in the Queen Street neighbourhood were built, the earth that was dug out was taken to the Nor' Loch. Now, as you know …' Robert and Malcolm winked at each other because Willie sounded so much like a teacher. '… the Nor' Loch lay between where we stay and the great hill on which Edinburgh Castle is built. So there used to be houses near the top of the Castle Hill and houses like ours much lower down with the loch in between, and no way of getting from one to the other without quite a long walk. Then it was decided to use all that huge amount of earth to build a road up to near the top of the Castle Hill. That was done and it's what we now call the Mound.'

'Some people call it Georgie Boyd's Mud Brig,' Malcolm said.

'And do you know who Geordie Boyd was?' ask Willie.

Robert's friend shook his head. 'I've no idea.'

'Well, I can tell you,' Robert's older brother said. 'When the houses on our side of the Nor' Loch were being built Geordie Boyd, a shopkeeper on the other side, used to pick his way across the earth that was dumped in the loch. And every time he crossed on the way back he took some of the debris and put it in the mud, so helping to build up the Mound.'

Robert was quiet as they walked home.

'If you do go to India,' he said after a while, 'I'll not need to go to see you.'

'Why not?' asked Willie.

His brother grinned. 'Because you're so good at describing things and explaining things that I'll know all about India from your letters without ever leaving Edinburgh!'

The Great Fire of Edinburgh

About 10 pm on 15th November 1824, flames were seen blazing through an engraver's window in a close off Edinburgh's High Street, and cries of 'Fire!' broke the quiet of the night. The horse-drawn fire engines arrived quickly but it took the firemen an hour to get their hoses up and running. By then the whole building was an inferno. A south-west wind soon had the adjoining house on fire. It was difficult to get the engines up the narrow close and within a terrifyingly short time the whole place was alight.

'Give us the hoses!' a voice yelled, from the top of the nearest building.

But nobody at ground level heard above the noise of the fire and the screaming of the crowd.

'The hoses!' all the men on the roof shouted at once. 'Give us the hoses!'

Knowing they could help by hosing down from above made their screams all the more desperate.

'The hoses! Give the hoses here!'

Their screams were not heard until it was too late to do any good, and the courageous men who had climbed to the top of the building raced back down again before they would be trapped by the spreading fire and burned to death.

The wind dropped and, in the still night air, flames and sparks flew upwards as though spouted from a huge volcano. The ash that fell as it cooled landed like snow on the fire-fighters, choking them as they breathed it in. People rushing to see the fire met a sight of utter horror. It seemed as if the whole world was burning, and the roar of buildings collapsing added to the fearsomeness of it. Men and women ran for their lives and children, confused and terrified, screamed until they could scream no more because their throats and lungs were full of the noxious ash and smoke.

About 1 am it began to rain and the wind changed, blowing the flames in the opposite direction. Firefighters didn't know which way to turn. Any good the heavy rain did was undone by the blustery wind. All night long men fought the flames, some collapsing with exhaustion only to pull themselves up again and go on with the job. At one point the Tron Church was entirely surrounded by burning buildings, but it stood there as though defying the fire to reach it. And it seemed as though it was going to escape when eventually almost the last of the flames was doused at 8 o'clock in the morning.

That's when it happened. A spark blown in the wind lodged in the Tron's wooden tower. Nobody noticed it beginning to smoulder. Nobody noticed the first tiny flame lapping the wood. And it was too late when a blood-curdling scream of, 'The Tron's on fire!' ripped through the air. The most powerful fire engine was soon on the job but nothing could prevent the church tower turning into a pyramid of flames. People watched in awe as the lead from the roof poured in molten streams down into the church. They gasped as the tower collapsed with a mighty crash. The huge bell that hung in the Tron's tower had crashed to the ground. The horror of it galvanised the firefighters to superhuman action and they managed to save the church.

A few hours later the three McCheyne brothers went to survey the devastation.

'I wonder how badly the church is damaged,' Robert said, as they walked quickly over the South Bridge.

Willie shook his head. 'They say the whole tower's away.'

'It would go up in minutes,' David said. 'It was built of wood, and too high for water to be hosed down on it.'

They marched along, all wanting to see the damage to their church and town. When they arrived it was just as they had been told. The church looked stark against the clear winter sky. And where the tower had stood there was just a tangle of charred wood pointing in all directions. Robert's mouth opened to say something then shut again. It was David who spoke first.

'It's hard to believe we were at a service there the day before yesterday.'

'But we'll never be at another one,' Willie added. 'The Tron's done for.'

The boys walked down one side of the building then up the other.

'I don't think it's done for at all,' suggested David. 'The main part of the building is stone. And although it's blackened by the fire I think it could be restored.'

A crowd had gathered from all over the city to see what there was to see. And a boy, who didn't seem to know much about Edinburgh at all, was pushed against the McCheynes.

'Is it the castle that's burned down?' he asked.

When Willie looked down and saw the lad, he smiled. 'No,' he said. 'The castle's quite safe. Do you want to see it?'

The boy nodded, and Willie lifted him on to his shoulders. 'Do you know where to look?'

'No,' the lad answered. 'I've never been right into the city before. I just came to see where the fire had been.'

'Look up the hill and tell me what you see.'

There are tall buildings all the way up to the top,' answered the boy.

'And what's right at the top?'

'I don't know, sir,' the lad said.

When the boy said 'sir' Willie put on his teacherish voice. Robert and David winked at each other and listened to what their brother had to say.

Willie pointed his new pupil in the right direction before continuing with his lesson, 'Look right up the hill to the end of the street and you'll catch just a glimpse of Edinburgh Castle.'

'Ooo! I can see it right enough!' the boy laughed. 'Please sir, what's down the other way? I think I can see water there.'

'That, young man, is the sea. But before you come to that, at the bottom of the hill is the Palace of Holyroodhouse. And the road we're standing on is called the Royal Mile. It runs from the Palace of Holyroodhouse at the bottom up to Edinburgh Castle at the top. Haven't you been taught this at school?' asked Willie.

'I've never been to school, sir,' he said. 'So I've not learned about these things.'

'What age are you?' Robert asked.

'I'm twelve,' answered the lad. 'And I'm a twine-winder by trade. I ran off when I heard about the fire because I wanted to see it so much.' Then he shook his head. 'But my master will beat me when I get back to work.'

Willie lifted the boy off his back and put him down beside Robert.

'I'd better go,' the young lad decided, and was off, pushing through the crowd to get back for his beating.

'That boy was older than I am,' Robert said, as they set off home. 'But he was much smaller and thinner.'

'That's because he's underfed,' Willie explained. 'And did you notice how pale he was and that his legs were bent outwards at the knees?'

His young brother nodded.

'He's probably been working as a twine-winder since he was five or six years old. In the winter he'll go to work before the sun rises and not finish until after dark. He'll get no daylight at all for several months of the year and not enough food. That's why he's pale and suffering from rickets.'

'What do twine-winders do?' asked Robert, as they walked towards home.

Willie, teacherish as ever, was the one to explain. 'Twine is only strong when several strands are wound together. So single strands are attached to a spindle then twisted together when the handle is turned.'

'And he does that from before daylight till after dark,' the lad whistled. 'That's terrible.'

They walked for a while in silence. Robert was thinking about the great fire... and about the boy they'd met and the beating he would get for running away from work to see the damage. Willie thought about rickets as they walked, and about the changes that would have to be made to prevent the disease which he knew was largely caused by poverty. And David thought about the Tron Church, about the times he'd worshipped God there and about all he had learned from the sermons. Then he wondered what Jesus would have done for the youngster they had just met.

'Did you notice his bare feet?' he asked his brothers.

Robert nodded. 'And his clothes were thin and ragged and wouldn't keep out the cold at all.'

'I wish I'd had some money with me that I could have

given the lad,' David fretted. 'Jesus wouldn't have let him go without helping him, and we did.'

'I don't know why you're studying to be a lawyer,' Robert said to David. 'You should be a minister instead.'

His brother smiled sadly, his mind still on the young boy. 'God needs Christian lawyers as well as Christian ministers,' he said. 'And it's maybe changes in the law that will make a difference to the likes of that young boy in the long run.'

When they turned into Queen Street, Eliza ran to meet them.

'I've been waiting for ages and ages for you to come back,' she said. 'Tell me all about the fire, and about the church... and about everything.'

Willie began to describe the burnt-out steeple. His brothers were amazed at the tiny details he remembered.

Two-and-a-half years later, when Robert was fourteen years old, he left Edinburgh High School for the last time. A big change was about to take place in his life for he was to go to university. Eventually the great day came.

'I'll have to watch I don't go to school by mistake, the High School and Edinburgh University are so close together.' He smiled at the thought.

As he walked along the South Bridge on his way to his first day as a student he passed several boys from the year below him in school.

'Hi, Robert!' one of them called across the road.

'He's Mr Robert Murray McCheyne now,' said another.

'That's right,' laughed Robert. 'Just you remember it!'

That morning was the beginning of eight years of university life.

'I think we should invite Robert McCheyne to join us for the evening,' a first-year student said to one of his friends. 'I've been watching him since we started university and he seems a decent fellow.'

'Go and ask him then,' the other young man said.

The two walked over to Robert, who was waiting for a horse-drawn carriage to pass before crossing the road.

'We're having a game of cards later and we wondered if you'd like to join us,' Robert was asked. 'There won't be any cheating.'

Robert McCheyne grinned. 'I'll come because of that, and thank you,' he laughed. 'I think cheating is mean and low but I enjoy an honest game of cards.'

They had a good time together, and began to meet up occasionally, sometimes to play cards, sometimes to go dancing, and sometimes just to talk.

'McCheyne's a decent fellow,' was what most people decided. He was truthful, loyal and a faithful friend. In fact, Robert was popular with lecturers and students alike. During his first three years at university he studied mainly Greek and Latin, but some other subjects too, including French, gymnastics and elocution. And he wrote poetry for pleasure as well as for university. Every year, on St Valentine's Day, he wrote a poem for whichever girl he was most fond of at the time.

'Let's walk to church together,' David suggested. 'The others will catch up.'

It was 1828, and the family had just started attending the newly built St Stephen's Church quite near their home. At first they walked in comfortable silence, then Robert spoke.

'Is there something on your mind?' he asked his brother.

'Yes, there is,' said David. 'But I don't want to hurt you.'

'Blurt it out then,' Robert suggested. 'And I promise not to be hurt.'

'You've always gone to church,' the older lad said, 'but have you asked Jesus to forgive your sins? I suppose what I'm asking is, are you really a Christian?'

His brother was quiet for a minute.

'I believe in God,' he said eventually, 'and I try to live the way the Bible teaches.'

'But that's not what I'm asking.'

'Well, then, I believe I am a Christian. In fact, I've been thinking about becoming a member of St Stephen's Church.'

Nothing else was said because the rest of the family caught up. A short time later Robert did become a church member, and he continued to try to live well while enjoying life with his friends. So interested was he in Christianity that McCheyne applied to study to be a minister.

'How are you enjoying studying theology?' David asked his younger brother, a few weeks into his new course.

'I love it,' replied Robert. 'Professor Chalmers really makes me think.'

'In what way?'

'It's hard to put into words,' Robert said. 'I'm beginning to realise that there's more to being a Christian than struggling to live a good life. You, for example, seem to know Jesus personally rather than just believe he exists.'

David smiled. 'I think I do know him personally. In fact, he's my friend as well as my Saviour.'

'I'm not there yet,' his young brother thought aloud. 'I'm convinced that Jesus is God, but I certainly couldn't call him my friend.'

'I pray that you will do one day,' said David.

'I know you do,' Robert nodded. 'You've been praying for me for years now, and somehow I feel that your prayers are not answered yet.'

'Just let me give you some advice,' the young man said. 'The Bible is God's word; read it and ask him to speak to you through it. And because you get to know people by talking to them, keep praying. That's my advice, Robert, read your Bible and keep praying.'

'I will,' his young brother promised. 'I'll do that.'

'Are you serious about going to India?' Robert asked his older brother, who was coming to the end of his medical course.

Willie nodded. 'Yes,' he replied. 'I'm absolutely serious. It's been in my mind so long that it's become part of me.'

'I remember you talking about it years ago,' said Robert. 'But I just can't imagine us not all being here together.'

'It has to come!' Willie laughed. 'We could all get married and move to different places. That's life.'

'I know, but I still can't imagine it.'

The older McCheyne grinned. 'Years ago you said you'd start saving so that if I did go to India you could come to visit me there. How much have you saved for the trip?'

Robert stood up and put his hand deep into his pocket. Putting all his money on the table, he counted it up.

'I have the princely sum of one shilling and seven pence three farthings. And I think that might just about hire me a carriage to see you off at Leith Docks, but no further!'

'Well you'd better start saving seriously because I've applied to serve as a doctor with the 54th Regiment, and if they accept me I'll be leaving for India in April.'

'Phew,' Robert whistled. 'That's less than a year from now. But at least David will still be here. Edinburgh lawyers are usually Edinburgh lawyers all of their lives. And Eliza won't be running off either.'

Willie was accepted for the 54th Regiment, and in April 1831 he set sail for India. The evening of the day he left was quiet and sad in the McCheyne household.

'India is so far away,' Eliza said, as they sat round the fire looking for comfort from its heat and finding none. 'Letters take weeks to come, and sometimes they don't arrive at all.'

'But the ones that do arrive will be interesting,' commented Robert. 'Willie's so good at describing things that reading his letters will be like seeing what he sees in India.'

'Are you all right?' Mr McCheyne asked his wife, noticing the weary look on her face.

'Yes,' she replied. 'I'm all right, just aware that the family will never be the same again.'

'Don't say that,' begged Eliza. 'It sounds so final.'

'You're very quiet, David,' said his father.

The young man smiled gently.

'I was just thinking about what the Bible says.'

'What's that?' Robert wanted to know.

'Jesus says that he is a friend who sticks closer than a brother. Willie may have gone, but the Lord has not.'

'Thank you,' said Mr McCheyne, 'I think that's helped us all.'

But Robert didn't feel helped. In his head he knew what David was saying was true, but in his heart he felt only a cold and heavy sadness.

David

'Are you free to go for a walk on Saturday?' Robert asked his older brother soon after Willie left for India.

David smiled. 'Yes,' he said. 'I'd like that. And the spring weather makes me want to be out in the hills.'

'Don't plan anything too strenuous,' Mrs McCheyne suggested. 'That cold seems to have settled on your chest and you'd be none the better for exhausting yourself.'

'I'll be careful,' David agreed. 'And I'm sure Robert will stop me from doing anything silly.'

Robert looked at his brother. 'Is it my imagination or is he looking even thinner than usual?'

Saturday came, and the brothers stuffed their picnic lunches into their pockets and headed off.

'Tell me about the walking holiday you're planning,' Robert said, as they went along.

David smiled. 'Well I hope to do some climbing in the Lake District. The fells are wild and challenging. And the views are magnificent.'

'If you can see them!' his brother laughed.

David looked puzzled. 'What do you mean?'

'I was remembering back to the time Malcolm and I walked over the hills from Dunkeld to Strathardle,' Robert explained. 'The view was lovely until the mist came down, and I mean right down. We couldn't see where we were going, let alone appreciate the view!'

'Scary,' commented David. 'And there was me telling Mum you'd look after me on the hills!'

Robert's memory was vivid. 'Eventually we realised it was dangerous to go on. One of us could have fallen and broken a leg and the other wouldn't have been able to find help. So we lay down in the heather under a great stone and thought we'd talk till morning.'

'And did you?'

'No' laughed his brother. 'We fell sound asleep and knew nothing till the bird-song woke us.'

They walked on in silence for a while but Robert's mind was still in Strathardle.

'You will be careful on the high fells?' he asked his brother.

It was David's turn to laugh. 'I'll be careful. I'll leave all the madcap adventures to you!'

'Let's stop for a rest,' David suggested, when they reached a fast-flowing stream. 'I'm needing a break.'

Robert sat down on a stone and took his picnic out of his pocket.

'It's not lunchtime yet but I'm going to have something to eat,' he said.

Quarter of an hour later David pulled himself to his feet. 'Let's get going; the day's too good to waste here.'

Normally they would have climbed straight up the hill then sat at the top planning the best way down. But as David seemed rather short of breath, and was prone to fits of coughing, they meandered uphill and rested when he felt like it. Coming down was a faster journey.

'There's a buzzard!' Robert whispered, pointing high in the air.

David looked up at the bird. 'Its wings are hardly moving,' he noticed. 'He must be hovering over his dinner.'

The pair stopped and watched the bird hovering. Then, with a flash of speed, it plummeted to the ground and was up again.

'It's got a young rabbit,' said Robert. 'And he's welcome to it. I prefer my rabbit in a stew.'

'Are you sure you're fit for a walking holiday?' Mr McCheyne asked his son. 'I heard you coughing during the night.'

'It's just what I'm needing,' David assured him. 'Edinburgh's not called Auld Reekie for nothing. I think the smoke and the fumes in the city are keeping this cold rumbling on. What I need is a holiday from work and some good fresh air in my lungs. Don't worry about me; I'll come back with more energy and some colour in my cheeks.'

So David went off to the Lake District where he climbed fells and ate picnics. He sat more often than he would normally have done and walked a little less. But, although he enjoyed his holiday, he was not really any better when he arrived back home. He did have more colour in his cheeks, but it was caused by fever rather than good health.

'I'm worried about David,' Mrs McCheyne told her husband soon afterwards. 'His eyes have lost their sparkle and that cough troubles him during the day and keeps him awake at night.'

Adam McCheyne nodded, but he was too choked to speak. Sometimes at work when he looked at David he seemed just a pale shadow of his old self. He'd lost one son to India, surely he wasn't going to lose another one to … to

death. Eliza and Robert also felt the cold hand of fear when
they looked at their older brother. And there was a sadness
in David that was new to him, a sadness that sent a chill up
Robert's spine.

'Don't let David die,' he prayed over and over and over
again. 'Please don't let him die.'

June became July, and by then it was clear to everyone
that the one they loved so much was dying. The long light
nights were spent beside him, reading the poems he loved,
singing hymns that seemed to comfort him. As the days of
early July passed, the gloom that had hung over David lifted
and a radiant joy took its place. It was as though every fear
left him as heaven became more real than earth. Robert
watched in awe as his brother prepared to die, though his
heart was in shreds. On 8th July 1831 joy flooded David
McCheyne's face as he died and went straight to heaven.
But the faces of those who sat round his bed were broken
by sorrow and grief. In the days that followed Robert lived
a mechanical life, doing what needed to be done but not
really being part of it.

'David gave me a Bible,' he remembered. 'And he asked
me to read it. I have done, but not as he did. I often saw him
reading his Bible, or going to his room to pray, when I've
been getting ready for some entertainment or other.'

With thoughts like that Robert punished himself. Then
the memory of David's joyful face came into his mind and
he felt a longing to share that joy. For years Robert had
been able to express himself best in poetry and that's what
he tried to do now. But in the end the last verse of the poem
about the brother he had lost was never written.

'I can't get David's face out of my mind,' he thought one
night as the clock chimed yet another hour. 'Although he

was dying he looked happier than I'd ever seen him before. I'd do anything to feel the joy he was feeling.'

He tossed and turned but still couldn't get to sleep.

'I am utterly miserable, yet I know David's happy in heaven. Would I go to heaven if I died tonight?' he wondered. And in his heart he knew he would not. He didn't have what David had had. He wasn't even certain what it was.

Robert was 18 years old and utterly miserable.

A year to the day after David's death, Robert opened his journal and began to write.

'On this morning last year came the first overwhelming blow to my worldliness. But only God knows how much he has turned it to good.'

Adam McCheyne was aware of a change in his young son. 'David's good example and joyful death seem to have made a big impact on Robert,' he said to his wife.

And she agreed. While others could see changes in Robert's life only God knew what was in his heart. But although he kept diaries none record the day he became a Christian. Like many others he may not have been able to pinpoint a date and time. What is certain is that, despite beginning to train for the ministry before putting his trust in Jesus, by the time Robert became a minister he was a believer and shared the joy he had so much envied in David.

Robert's new faith spurred him into action and he was soon doing mission work in the old part of Edinburgh.

'For years I've looked at these tall buildings,' he told a friend, 'but it never occurred to me to go into them and visit the people there who don't know that Jesus has died to save them.'

He tramped along the Lawnmarket, visiting up the narrow closes that went off on either side. Climbing the dark staircases he remembered back to 1824 and the Great Fire that had raged through the area. And the poverty he found tore at his heart.

'There are children huddled together to keep warm,' he told his mother. 'The poor things are nearly naked.' His voice caught in his throat with emotion.

Mrs McCheyne looked at Robert as he left the room, and worried.

'He's wearing himself out with all this visiting,' she decided. 'I'm going to write to Willie and ask him to send a letter back to Robert advising him to be more careful.'

She picked up her pen but put it down again to wipe away her tears.

'I just couldn't bear to lose him,' she said to herself. 'I couldn't bear it.'

She looked at the paper and wondered how to phrase what she wanted to say. Deciding on the words, she began, 'Write Robert some good advice. Tell him to pay attention to his health.'

And his mother sighed deeply the following Saturday morning when she heard her son leaving the house at 5.45 am. 'Why does he have to meet his friends so early on a Saturday morning?' she wondered. 'Surely they could discuss things at a more reasonable time of day.'

Unaware that the noise of leaving had wakened his mother Robert strode happily along Queen Street. 'I just love these early morning meetings,' he thought. 'They're the best possible start to the weekend.'

He smiled as he walked. 'Mind you, some of the others don't like it quite so much. But I've always been an early bird; I even wrote a university essay on the benefits of getting up very early.'

The following Monday Robert was up at the crack of dawn, not to meet with his friends, but to pray.

'This is when I meet with my best friend,' he thought, as he knelt down to pray.

Then, out of the blue, something came to his mind that warmed his heart.

'That's what David said that day on our way to church! He said that Jesus was his Saviour and his friend, and that he would pray it would be the same for me some day. Well, his prayers have been answered even though he's not here to know it. I've lost a brother I loved very much, but Jesus said that he was the friend who sticks closer than a brother.'

And as he spoke to the Lord, Robert McCheyne thanked him for all those who had prayed for him over the years, and for hearing and answering their prayers.

'Have you finished your studying for the night?' Eliza asked Robert, when he came into the sitting-room.

'Yes,' he replied. 'Is there something you want me to do?'

His sister laughed. 'Yes, there is. I've been sitting here at the window trying to draw the view and I just can't get it right. You're a much better artist than I am so will you help me?'

'Flattery will get you everywhere!' Robert laughed. 'Let's see what you've done.'

The pair sat down on the window seat and with a very few pencil strokes Robert saved the picture.

'It was your perspective that was wrong,' he explained. 'The things in the distance were just too big and that threw the whole thing out. Try drawing the view in that direction.'

Eliza turned round and looked further towards the east

then began to sketch. Robert also began sketching, but not the view from the window. He drew his sister drawing. The evening light reached her forehead as she bent forward and threw the lower part of her face into the shade. Holding his pencil on the slant the young man shaded carefully, leaving the highlights with no shading at all. Then he drew the window frame behind her, and with the lightest of touches gave an impression of the view beyond, right over to the Lomond Hills in Fife. Neither Eliza nor her brother noticed the door opening or their mother coming in.

'What a lovely scene,' she said. 'Two artists at work, one drawing the other as she draws.'

'You know what you should do then,' laughed Robert. 'You should draw me drawing Eliza drawing the view from the window!'

Mrs McCheyne smiled. 'If I could, I would. But I can't!'

'Robert will teach you,' Eliza said. 'He's an expert on perspective!'

Her mother shook her head. 'From my perspective I'm too old a dog to be learning new tricks. But I would enjoy looking at both your sketches.'

The fire was on, the room was warm and the day's work was done. So Mrs McCheyne and her grown-up children relaxed and enjoyed their evening together.

'Your one first,' she said, opening up Eliza's folder of drawings and working her way through them before moving on to Robert's sketchbook.

'I like the way you've collected them together,' his mother said. 'It's like looking through an album of your life.'

Robert showed her drawing after drawing and explained where and what they were.

'That's the house in Dublin Street,' he said, then he laughed. 'I did it quite recently, not before we moved here when I was six!'

'You were all born in Dublin Street,' Mrs McCheyne sighed. 'Willie, then David, then you,' she said, smiling at Eliza. 'Then there was little Isabella who died before you were born, Robert. And then of course yourself, the baby of the family.'

'Some baby!' his sister laughed. 'A few months from now your baby will be a minister!'

Turning over the pages Robert came to some sketches of Clarencefield.

'There's Aunt Dickson feeding her hens, and there are the four cows she's so proud of,' Mrs McCheyne said, smiling at the thought of her sister.

'And that's the family,' said Robert quietly, as he handed her a set of drawings. They were all there: the parents and all their children apart from Isabella. The drawings were profiles, even his self-portrait.

'What I don't understand,' laughed Eliza, 'is how you managed to draw your own profile. How could you possibly see the side of your head to draw it?'

'Good question,' Robert said. 'And one for which I don't have a good answer!'

1835 was a busy year for Robert Murray McCheyne. His university studies finished in the late spring and the following months were taken up with preparing and preaching sermons to his professors and churchmen. There were also more examinations to be passed before he could be ordained as a minister of the Church of Scotland. Eventually all that had to be done was to preach a trial sermon in public. It was decided that he should do this in Annan Church in Dumfriesshire, and it was with a mixture of anticipation and anxiety that he set out. His sermons passed the test, and on 1st July 1835 Robert Murray McCheyne was licensed to preach.

'David prayed that I'd become a preacher,' he thought, as he rode along the road to Clarencefield, 'I just wish he'd been here to see today.'

When he arrived at his aunt's home the hens scuttled away from the horse's hooves, and the noise brought Aunt Dickson running. From the expression on her nephew's face she knew things had gone well in Annan.

'There are newly-baked scones and oatcakes waiting for you, and crowdie cheese and raspberry jam as well,' she told her visitor as he tied up his horse.

Robert laughed aloud. 'Have you left me to collect the eggs?'

'I have indeed! You may be a licensed preacher but you're still my egg-collector in chief!'

'It's going to be strange hearing you preach in Ruthwell,' Aunt Dickson said, as they drank their tea together. 'And a real privilege too. Have you any other preaching engagements arranged?'

'Yes,' said Robert. 'I'm speaking in Leith, near Edinburgh, next Saturday and Sunday, which is why I can only stay here for a few days.'

'You're having a busy start to your ministry,' commented his aunt, 'and I imagine it will go on that way.'

Having preached for the first time in the church he knew so well as a child, the young man relaxed for a day before heading back home.

'I wonder where home will be soon,' he thought. Would

it be in Perthshire, where he and Malcolm had bedded down for the night in the fog? Or in Inverness-shire where he had climbed with David? Or perhaps in Edinburgh itself. 'I've no idea where it will be,' he told the horse, 'but God knows already.'

Several ministers invited Robert to be their assistant, but only one of them seemed right.

'Mr John Bonar has asked me to go to Larbert and Dunipace,' he told his family a month or two later. 'And I feel that's where God wants me.'

'Show me on the map where that is,' said Eliza, unfolding a cloth-backed map of Central Scotland on the dining-room table.

Robert traced a road with his finger. 'You go west out of Edinburgh,' he told his sister, 'to Linlithgow and past Linlithgow Palace, then a little north of west for about the same distance again to Larbert.'

'How far is it from here?' she asked.

Taking a ruled measure, Robert laid it on the map. 'It's about 25 miles as the crow flies.'

'It's a pity you're not a crow then,' teased Eliza. 'You'll just have to do it on horseback.'

Her brother grinned. 'I can't think of any better way.'

Travels with Tully

Robert slowed his horse and reined him in to the side of the road.

'Well, Tully,' he said, 'what do you think of your new home? It seems to me that this is just the ideal place for a man and his horse.'

Giving the creature a playful slap on the side, McCheyne nudged him with his heels and they were off again.

'Let's go along the River Carron to the church. We're not meeting Mr Bonar there till 2 o'clock.'

As they picked their way along the riverside the banks on either side grew steeper. Robert looked around at the unfamiliar countryside that made up the united parishes of Larbert and Dunipace where he was to spend a year assisting the minister, Rev John Bonar.

'Larbert's very different from Dunipace,' he thought, as he rode from one to the other. 'Most of the Dunipace people are still traditional farmers, each with his own small croft. But since the Carron Ironworks opened in the middle of last century Larbert has become one of the largest industrial areas of Scotland.'

They were nearly at the church before Robert noticed it high above him on his left.

'We should have left the river earlier,' he told Tully. 'It would have saved you this steep climb up to the church. Not to worry, I'll get off and we'll climb it together.'

Having dismounted, Robert took his horse by the rein

and they climbed up the hillside to the church. As the young minister was there before Bonar, he tied Tully to a tree and walked round the churchyard.

'Although the church and churchyard are quite new there have been a lot of burials here already.' The few headstones told their own stories and the more frequent wooden crosses marked the graves of the poor. There was even a small iron memorial set to the memory of someone who had worked in the Carron Ironworks.

'What a lot of children die as infants,' Robert thought sadly. 'And I've seen a couple where it seems mothers died in childbirth and their babies died too.' He walked on. 'I'm puzzled by some of the names because they don't sound Scottish at all.'

Suddenly Robert realised he was not alone. John Bonar was standing just behind him.

'Each one tells a story,' Mr Bonar said. 'That one there, for example, to the memory of the McLuckie children who died in infancy. There were four children; the oldest would have been about five when the measles struck. None survived.'

'What do you say to a family like that?' Robert asked.

The minister looked at the rough wooden cross as he spoke. 'I tell them that Jesus understands their heartbreak because his own heart was often broken here on earth. And I try to point them gently to the Saviour who died on just such a wooden cross so that they might have their sins forgiven and go to heaven when they die. There is nothing else worth saying when death strikes with that violence.'

Mr Bonar stood in silence at the children's grave and his assistant knew he was praying for the family so sadly torn apart.

'Right then,' said John Bonar. 'Let me tell you about the work we'll be doing together. The church here was built 15 years ago and the one at Dunipace was finished just last year. This one seats 640 and the other is a bit smaller. Services are held in both each Sunday, and we'll divide them between us. Then there is visiting. Of course we visit homes where there is sickness and death. But what I really want you to do is to visit the people who don't come to church at all. Since the Ironworks opened people have come from all over Scotland to work here, and others have even come from England to find jobs.'

'That explains the English names in the churchyard,' Robert commented. 'I wondered how they came to be here.'

'Before the Ironworks opened there were about 400 people in this area; now there are about 6,000,' said Mr Bonar. 'Many of them are never inside the door of the church and some who do come sleep right through the sermon.'

'There's certainly plenty of work for us both here,' thought McCheyne.

'Yesterday was my first Sunday,' Robert wrote to his father a few days later. 'I preached to a big congregation in Larbert and Mr Bonar took the service in Dunipace. At the end of the Larbert service a man asked me to visit one of his workers who was dying. As there was plenty of time to do that before Mr Bonar returned from Dunipace I went to see the old man. But he died just before we arrived. I'm told that he was a fine Christian so I was able to comfort the family with the sure hope that the one they had lost was in heaven with Jesus. We rode back to the manse through beautiful autumn colours and Tully's hooves kicked the dry leaves in the air. Mr Bonar preached in Carron School in the afternoon and I went along.

He spoke so well - but for an hour-and-a-half! He told me that sometimes workers fall asleep during his sermons. Now I understand why! It's not that his sermons are boring, it's just that they are far too long!'

Robert was not many weeks in his new job when his sister came to visit. As they sat in his room talking Eliza watched her brother carefully.

'He looks tired,' she thought. 'I suspect that because he's not got a wife to look after him he just works all the time.'

'Tell me about the people here,' she asked, hoping that Robert hadn't guessed what she was thinking!

'My dear people,' sighed Robert, as he leant back in his chair. 'Where do I begin?'

Eliza sat quietly as Robert gathered his thoughts.

'Mr Bonar and I share the work in both Larbert and Dunipace, but as most people are in Larbert most of the work is too. The Carron Ironworks employ many hundreds of men and children. Then there are the miners at Kinnaird who are my special responsibility and my special treasure.'

Eliza asked if that was because they were nice folk.

Robert looked at his sister. 'In the main they are dirty, rough and ignorant. And as far as knowing about the Lord, they might as well be in the middle of the darkest jungle. But underneath it all they are kind folk to those who are kind to them. And I hope that befriending them will let me introduce them to the best friend of all, the Lord Jesus.'

'And tell me about Mr Bonar,' said Eliza.

McCheyne grinned. 'He's a great man to work for. He must be the most conscientious minister in Scotland as far as visiting goes.'

'Why do you say that?'

Laughing, Robert said, 'There's not a Carroner's wife who takes a pain in her head or foot but she has a minister at her door weekly till she's well again!'

'I get the picture,' giggled Eliza.

They sat, one on either side of the fire, drinking tea and enjoying each other's company.

'Tell me about Mr Bonar's preaching,' Eliza said. 'Is he as good a preacher as he is a visitor?'

'He preaches really good sermons,' Robert told her. 'But he preaches for too long, usually about an hour-and-a-half.'

'Many preachers do that,' commented his sister. 'What's so wrong with sermons that length?'

'I'll tell you what. The people here labour very long hours. Those who work on farms begin when the sun rises in the morning and finish when it sets at night. The men in the Ironworks do the same. In the winter they never see the sun at all. Even the children work every daylight hour.'

Eliza looked troubled.

'Yes,' Robert assured her. 'Children work like slaves. And because they are underfed, and in the dark much of the time, they are small for their ages and prone to catching whatever diseases hit the area. When measles or typhoid sweeps up the valley they leave many dead children in their wake. And when you hear the coughing you know some of them have tuberculosis.'

'Poor lambs,' his sister said.

'So you see,' Robert added, 'most of our people are so exhausted when they arrive in church that they're sleepy anyway so there's little hope of them staying awake for an hour-and-a-half.'

'How long do you preach for?'

'I've thought a lot about that,' McCheyne answered. 'And I've decided not to speak for more than 35 minutes. I think most will stay awake that long.'

When Eliza arrived back in Edinburgh she told her parents about Larbert and Dunipace and about the poor people Robert served. Then, seeing the concern in her mother's eye when she mentioned tuberculosis, the young woman changed the mood by describing her brother's lodgings. 'It's a large room,' she said, 'and it's crammed full of furniture. There is a bed, two chests of drawers, three tables, six immense chairs and Robert's two trunks! It's all right until you try to walk from one end to the other then it's like an obstacle course! It's just as well that he's athletic!'

Within two months of arriving in Larbert Robert had developed a harsh cough that would not go away. He worked on despite it until he could work no more. Afraid that he was reaching a point of collapse, it was agreed that he would return to Edinburgh for a few weeks until he was better. Mrs McCheyne hovered outside her son's bedroom while the doctor examined him, and she was there and waiting to hear what he had to say when he came out.

'Is it tuberculosis?' the woman asked, so giving voice to her worst fear.

The doctor nodded. 'Yes, I'm afraid he does have the beginnings of tuberculosis but the tissue of his lungs seems unaffected, though he has little use of his right lung. But he's a young man and very determined,' the doctor concluded kindly. 'Just nurse him carefully and get him on his feet again.'

As Robert lay in bed he thought deep thoughts. 'I have tuberculosis and I might die of it,' he decided truthfully. 'But what an opportunity that gives me. I won't waste time because I don't know how much time I have left. And those I visit or preach to could be dying as well. So from now on I'll preach as a dying man to dying men and when I visit I'll do the same. Meanwhile, I must write to some of the sick folk in Larbert telling them that I'm praying for them.'

There was a quiet knock on his door then Mrs McCheyne came in with a cup of tea. 'You'll not be needing these just yet,' she said, taking the half-written letter out of his hand and replacing it with the teacup.

Robert grinned. 'You can't keep an eye on me all the time,' he teased his mother.

'No,' she agreed. 'But when I can't, Eliza will!'

Robert recovered sufficiently to return to Larbert and to work. And when he arrived it was to discover that he wasn't the only one who was ill. Workers, their lungs weakened by the conditions in which they laboured, took colds that went to their chests and became pneumonia. Coal miners and the children who worked down the mine, their lungs already black with dust, were often the first to become poorly. Sick-visiting and funerals took up much of the ministers' time. But the spring came eventually and things began to improve. Tully and Robert were known throughout the area because, as the locals said, 'they were forever on the road.' The nosier folk watched to see where Tully was tethered to know where illness had struck. But when the horse found its way to their own post they discovered that they didn't need to be sick to have a visit from the minister. Their souls were good enough reason for Robert.

'8th July 1836,' Robert wrote in his journal. 'It is five years today since David died, but although he is absent from his body he is present with the Lord. And he knows more about the Lord now than every Christian on earth put together.'

McCheyne lay back in his chair and thought about his brother in heaven. 'The Bible says there is no death or mourning or crying or pain in heaven,' he remembered. 'I'm glad all these things are behind David now and that he is where they can't touch him.'

He thought of the day's visiting he had done, of the sorrow and sickness he'd met and of the mourning in the hearts of the people whose loved ones had died.

'It's what is in heaven that's important,' Robert smiled. 'David is with every other Christian who has ever lived and died and they're all enjoying the presence of the Lord in wonderful ways that I can't begin to imagine.'

A feeling of joy and tenderness flooded the young man. 'I wonder how long it will be before I go to heaven,' he found himself thinking. His brush with tuberculosis was very fresh in his mind.

Soon after starting work again Robert was offered a rent-free house in Carronvale which was in the part of the parish where he did most work. Mrs McCheyne was especially pleased about the move as it meant that Eliza could live there from time to time and help her brother.

Robert kept a note of the homes he visited and the reception he received. His notes were so detailed that we can visit the miners' homes in Red Row with him.

'John Hunger, No 22. He, not at home. She, stout woman with sensible face. Spoke of her four dead children.

Three still alive. I spoke to her about Jesus' words, "I stand at the door and knock." Altogether a decent woman. Husband to be at meeting.'

'James Rankin, No 23. He at work. Wife hoarse-speaking, attentive, understanding. Two live children; three dead. Told of Jesus healing a sick child.'

'Alexander McLuckie, No 24. Red-haired man; honest, inquiring face. Wife, clever. Four girls. Asked the little girls questions then spoke to them all about Jesus' words, "Suffer the little children to come to me."'

'Alexander Hunter, No 39. Intelligent man. Met with wife in another house. Decent family. Boy and a girl, and they lost another three. Spoke about the gospel being hidden treasure. Hunter suggested we pray for the workers underground.'

'Widow Hunter, No 40. Wicked face, but the old woman has had much trouble. Daughter lame. Told her about Jesus looking for the lost sheep. She said she was grateful for what I said, but I knew she wasn't. Told me to come any time I was passing.'

'Peter Rae, No 44. Ill-looking man. Hard, hard woman. A large family of mocking girls. Talked about the need for pardon and a new heart. Their hearts are like iron, cold and hard.'

So the young minister went on knocking door after door after door, speaking in every home about the Lord Jesus, and encouraging people to believe before it was too late.

Robert was sitting in his study in Carronvale working on a sermon when Eliza brought him an apple.

'You need all the fruit you can get to keep you healthy,' she told her brother, before asking what he was doing.

'I'm just writing out my notes for Sunday's sermons.'

'Some ministers write their sermons out in full and read them,' Eliza said. 'But you only take one page with headings on it, don't you?'

'That's right,' Robert agreed. 'I don't like having sermons read to me, and I don't think I could read a sermon either. But I always take this with me.' He handed Eliza a sheet of paper with a list of six or seven points and nothing more.

'I'd be afraid I'd forget what I wanted to say if that's all I had with me,' the young woman giggled. 'It's just as well I'm not the minister!'

The following Sunday morning Robert put his sermon notes into his pocket before saddling Tully and heading off to take the service in Dunipace. When he arrived there he couldn't find his notes.

'The sheet of paper must have fallen out of my pocket,' he thought anxiously.

He tried to relax and think through his sermon points. Because he had prepared so well they came back to him easily. And that day, in the pulpit of Dunipace Church, Robert McCheyne changed his style of preaching. He discovered that if he was well prepared he could speak very much more freely with no notes at all.

'Have you heard about the lad from the village who has run away from home?' Mr Bonar asked his assistant at the beginning of August 1836. Robert listened to the story and felt for the young man who wanted to enjoy life more than his parents were allowing him to do. Knowing where the lad was staying, Robert decided to write him a letter. 'Not long ago I was just like you,' he wrote. 'I enjoyed the games you enjoy and read the books you're now reading. The same young blood flowed in my veins as is flowing in yours, and I dreamed the same dreams. Although you think of me as the minister I'm not old and grey-headed. In some ways I'm as much of a boy as you are and as fond of life and happiness.' McCheyne sat back in his chair and thought before continuing.

'I don't suppose that many boys were as happy as I was before I was a Christian. I enjoyed life to the full.' But even as he wrote the words Robert knew that the joy that came when he trusted in Jesus was far and above anything he had known before. So he told the lad about his brother and how David's life and death had led him to Jesus.

As Robert's time in Larbert and Dunipace drew towards its close the church that showed most interest in calling him to be its minister was St Peter's in Dundee. Several young men were being considered, including two of Robert's best friends. McCheyne wrote to his father about it. 'I'm not concerned about the outcome,' he said. 'God will lead the right man there. It's curious that my two best friends are my 'rivals' for St Peter's! I've no doubt that each of us wishes one of the other two to get it. And if the people have any sense they'll choose Andrew Bonar who is the best young minister I know.'

Andrew had been at university with Robert and he was a relation of John Bonar of Larbert. The people of St Peter's made up their own minds and they called Robert to be their minister. Andrew was called to a church near enough to Dundee that the two young men would be able to meet quite often. John Bonar knew he would miss his assistant very much indeed, and that the people in the area would too. He wrote, 'Robert McCheyne is greatly loved and delighted in by my people, and the longer they know him and the more they see of him, the better they love him.' Mr Bonar's heart was not the only one to be sad when Robert and Tully rode out of Larbert for the last time.

Rescued from a Tree

It was on 14th August 1836 that Robert preached in St Peter's Church in Dundee for the first time and the congregation seemed to know right away that they wanted him to be their minister, so much so that they didn't ask the other candidates to come at all! In the two months that followed before he moved to Dundee he tried to find out as much about the city as he could.

'The population of Dundee is about 51,000,' McCheyne told his friend Hugh. 'Some are hugely rich, especially those whose businesses import jute. You should see their mansions! It's just a pity that many of the men and women that work for them are forced to live in hovels because they are so poorly paid. Some of the places I've seen defy description... but I'll try to describe them all the same. The buildings were just thrown up and they hold together where they can. They are so cold that rags are forced into the cracks to keep the cold east wind out. The interiors of their homes are so blackened by soot that it's impossible to say what's soot and what's dirt. And the smell! How these poor people can bear it I really don't know.'

Hugh listened and imagined the scene.

Sitting back on his chair Robert tried to find words that would convey what it was like to be poor in Dundee.

'I thought that the people of Larbert suffered, but at least they had clean water from the River Carron and the streams round about, not to mention their wells. In Dundee many draw their water from the stagnant pools of cooling water discharged from factories or from wells full of the stuff. Not only that, their toilet pits are often dug right beside the water supply because it's all the space they have. It doesn't bear thinking about, but it means that what seeps through from the toilet pits is drawn up again from the wells and used for drinking water! It's no wonder the smell is so obnoxious and that cholera cuts its deadly swathe through these areas of the city with sickening regularity. The appalling thing about cholera is that it takes people so suddenly. I heard of a man who became ill at eleven o'clock one morning and was dead by two that same afternoon!'

'Cholera is a dreadful scourge,' Hugh agreed. 'And it can take whole families.'

'It's not the only one either,' his friend added. 'There's typhus fever and smallpox and countless other diseases troubling my poor folk.'

Hugh smiled. 'He's not even there yet, and he thinks of these folk as his own. That's just typical of McCheyne. He'll love them even if it means visiting homes where he's likely to catch diseases himself.'

Standing up, Hugh suggested they went for a ride. 'The horses could do with some exercise and so could we.'

As the two young men rode along the banks of the River Carron Robert signalled to his companion to stop.

'Round this bend in the river we'll probably come across a heron fishing. He's usually there at this time of day. It's great to watch and a novelty for a city man like you. Let's leave the horses here and go on foot so not to disturb him.'

McCheyne was right enough. The heron was standing stock-still in the water, more like a statue than a bird. For minutes there was no movement whatever then, quick as a flash, his beak stabbed the water and brought up a fish.

'Phew!' Hugh smiled. 'It didn't stand a chance!'

And the heron having swallowed the fish in a gulp was once again standing ready to pounce.

'So much for the delights of the countryside,' laughed Hugh. 'It wasn't very delightful for that fish.'

'Is there much fishing done out of Dundee?' Hugh asked, as they strode back to their horses.

Tully whinnied at the sight of her master; he always seemed glad to see him.

'Oh yes,' said Robert. 'There's a big fleet of boats and others come and go in season with the fish. It's quite a sight when the boats come in and the fishwives start gutting the catch.'

'That must be a freezing cold job,' shivered Hugh.

'So cold that they lose the feeling in their fingers and have to wrap their hands up in rags to stop them cutting themselves. But you should hear them singing as they work. I suppose it keeps their mind off the cold.'

'What else comes into the harbour there?'

'Jute's the main thing, but there is much else besides. It's a very busy port.'

'I've never been to Dundee,' Hugh commented. 'Tell me about it as we ride.'

Robert and his friend mounted their horses and set out at walking pace for Carronvale.

'Dundee is in a lovely situation,' Robert began. 'As you know, it's on the north banks of the Firth of Tay. From the city you look over the Tay to Fife. There's a ferry from Dundee to Tayport and it's kept very busy.'

They rode in silence for a few minutes.

'It's strange,' Robert went on, 'Where I was brought

up looked north over the Firth of Forth to Fife, now I'm going to live in Dundee where I'll look south over the Firth of Tay to Fife! It seems I'm going to spend most of my life looking at Fife from one direction or the other!'

'And what's the city itself like?' asked Hugh.

'It's quite an interesting place,' his friend said. 'Dundee Law is its highest point and the view from the top is wonderful'

'And where's St Peter's? Is it on Dundee Law?' Hugh wondered.

'No, it's near the Tay on the road that runs from Dundee west to Perth. The area is a poor one. Many people who've come to Dundee looking for factory work live there.'

Robert stopped speaking, and looked into the far distance.

'What are you seeing?' asked Hugh.

'I may be wrong,' Robert said. 'But I think those lads over there are in trouble.'

Nudging their horses to a canter the two young men rode in the direction of a little group of boys gathered at the foot of an old beech tree.

'Is everything all right?' asked Robert when they reined their horses to a stop.

They boys looked at one another, then the tallest spoke.

'No sir,' he said, recognising the minister. 'Jimmy's stuck up the tree. We were looking for birds' eggs and he climbed too far along that branch and now he can't turn round and he's scared to crawl backwards in case the branch breaks.'

Robert was off his horse like a shot and much to the boys' surprise he was up the tree as quickly as they could have climbed it.

'Hold on,' he told the lad. 'We'll soon have you down.'

Surveying the branches for safety, McCheyne climbed to the branch below the one Jimmy was on.

'Pull your legs up on the branch,' he instructed. 'That'll spread your weight. Now, tuck your ankles over the branch and ease yourself back a tiny bit.'

'The branch will break if I move,' the boy whined.

'Not if you move how I tell you.'

Robert climbed out beyond the boy and showed him exactly what he wanted him to do.

'That's right,' he encouraged. 'Bend your elbows as far as you can and push yourself backwards.'

Jimmy did what he was told.

'Now straighten your legs again and hold the branch tight with your ankles.'

Three more moves, and a very relieved young man felt his feet touch the trunk of the tree.

'Good lad!' McCheyne said. 'But I think you should give up egg-collecting. It's a very dangerous hobby!'

Scrambling down to his friends, Jimmy grinned widely.

'Yes sir,' he said to Robert, who was swinging to the ground. 'I'd best do that.'

'You may be a thin chap and pale at the best of times but you keep yourself fit!' laughed Hugh, as they set off again.

Robert smiled. 'I've always loved gymnastics. But what were we talking about before we were so excitingly interrupted?'

'I think you were going to tell me about the area around St Peter's Church.'

'Oh yes, I remember. Dundee has grown by 20,000 people in just 14 years. So if everyone in the city went to church a huge number wouldn't be able to get in the doors. It's not that there would be standing room only; there would be no room. So it was decided to build a church in Hawkhill where there was no place of worship at all. Land was bought on the Perth Road and the church built. Hawkhill runs uphill from the Tay and it's quite steep in places. The houses in the area vary a great deal but most are poor dwellings. There are one or two streets where wealthier folk stay.'

'Is the church very beautiful?' Hugh asked.

'No,' his friend admitted. 'It's quite plain. The building sits off the road and the land between it and Perth Road will be the churchyard. St Peter's itself is a squarish building with ten arched windows on either side, in two rows one above the other. It's nice and bright inside but not at all ornate. There wasn't the money for that but I don't like fancy church buildings. They can be a real distraction.'

'Where will you be staying?'

Robert smiled. 'Just along the road from the church there's a narrow lane running steeply downhill to the Tay. It's called Strawberry Bank. Eliza and I will be living down there.'

'What a lovely address! Rev Robert Murray McCheyne, Strawberry Bank, Dundee!'

'That's Tully's new address too,' laughed Robert. 'His stable is just across the lane from where we'll be staying!'

The two young men had arrived back at Robert's lodgings. They gave their horses a brush down before stabling them for the night.

'By the way,' said McCheyne. 'St Peter's can hold 1,175 people. So if you ever see your way to coming to a service there will only be room for 1,174 others.'

'It could be a tight squeeze then,' Hugh laughed.

When the time came for 23-year-old Robert to move to Dundee he travelled by Perth and stayed overnight with a friend not far from his destination. The following morning he was up early as usual studying his Bible and praying about the big day ahead. It was 24th November 1835 and he was about to be ordained as a minister and inducted to St Peter's. Although McCheyne arrived at the church very early, crowds of people were there before him. And a mini crowd of children had gathered to find out what was going on and to see if there was anything in it for them.

'Hey mister!' a little scamp named Geordie shouted. 'What's all the fuss about?'

People ignored the boy as they entered the church, but Robert didn't. Crouching down till he was the same height as the child, he explained that he was going to be made minister of the new church.

'How does that happen?' the little lad asked.

McCheyne smiled. 'Grown-up folk would say that I was about to be ordained and inducted.'

'Ouch!' Geordie said. 'That sounds painful!'

'I hope not!' Robert laughed. 'All the local ministers will be there. One of them will ask me questions about what I believe and I'll make special promises.'

'What kind of promises?' they wanted to know.

'I'll promise only to teach the people what God says in the Bible. Then all the ministers will put their right hands on me and set me apart to be a minister. When that's done I'll be ordained.'

'What about being conducted? You said you'd be conducted too?'

Robert smiled kindly. 'I think I said I'd be inducted.

71

That means that I'll be made minister of St Peter's.'

'Are you coming to stay in Dundee then?' a girl asked.

'I am indeed. And if you live near here it means I'll be one of your neighbours.'

She looked pleased. 'Can we come and see you after you've come to live in the church?'

Laughing aloud, McCheyne explained that he wouldn't be living in the church, but in Strawberry Bank, just along the Perth Road.

'But I'd better be going,' he explained. 'Or I'll be late for the service, and that wouldn't be a good start!'

Robert was taken to the minister's room at the back of the church until it was time for the service to begin. When he came out and into the church he discovered that the building was crammed full of people. Feeling quite overwhelmed the young man bowed his head and prayed that St Peter's would not only be full on this special occasion but on ordinary Sundays too. The service over, the new minister and sixty others went to a hotel for dinner and some formal speeches and a little crowd of filthy urchins were there to see them off. They were pleased to see that their new friend kept grand company.

A few days later Rev Robert Murray McCheyne sat down at his desk to write his weekly letter to his parents. His brother Willie was home on leave from India so the letter was addressed to him too.

'Dear Dad, Mum and Willie,

Eliza and I have been here for a week now and we are beginning to get to know the place. We are well settled in Strawberry Bank though the house is a bit smoky. Maybe that's because Dundee is full of smoke from all the factory chimneys, or maybe the chimney needs cleaning. Tully also has comfortable quarters just across the lane from us. When we come out the house into the lane we have either a steep walk up to Perth Road or a steep walk down towards the Tay. The river is just a few minutes walk away. Tully prefers going up the way as the lane can be slippery in the rain. He'll get used to it.

We have both been very busy,' he went on. 'Eliza is organising the household beautifully. If fact, if I sit still very long I think I'll find myself being dusted! I've already conducted one wedding and visited a good number of sick people. This week I hope to get to know the elders. They look a decent bunch of men. They'll need to be. Dundee's a dark city and I don't just mean it's smoky. You just have to walk along the road to see the dark side of it. Men who hardly earn enough to feed their families spend much of what they earn in the beer shops on the way home. There's enough to keep me busy for as long as I'm in Dundee. And I've no doubt that Eliza will be kept busy looking after me.'

'What are you doing?' Eliza asked one day soon after they had settled in their new home.

Robert had a sheet of paper on his desk and he seemed to be drawing a pattern on it. He pointed to a double line on the sheet.

'That,' he said, 'is Strawberry Bank, and there is our house.'

Tracing with his finger along the lines he had drawn he showed his sister where the church was, and the baker and the butcher.

'Why do you need to draw a map?' queried Eliza. 'You're beginning to know your way around quite well.'

'Look at this,' McCheyne said, taking another sheet of paper out of his drawer. 'This is one of the narrow streets off Perth Road, the one I've been visiting this week. Here you see I've tried to draw in all the little flats in the tenements. And I've noted who lives in each of them.'

'I can see that's useful,' the young woman said. 'But it's going to be an awful lot of work.'

Nodding in agreement Robert said it would be worthwhile.

'Say I visit the Macleod family in 10 Duncan's Land. Next time I go they'll expect me to remember everyone in the family. And if I can't remember they'll feel I don't care. Or if I get a message that Mr Macleod is dying and wants to speak to me I can't go around knocking on all the doors at 10 Duncan's Land looking for him. So the best way to keep track of everyone is by drawing detailed maps and indicating who lives where.'

'I can see that,' Eliza agreed. 'And I'm glad you've always been good at art. Most people wouldn't know where to start such a major project.'

Midway through January Robert and his sister wakened to a very different view of Dundee. Instead of looking smoky and black the city was glistening white under a deep blanket of snow. Something of the child was always inside McCheyne, and it may be that he walked further that day than he needed just for the joy of it. Not surprisingly Eliza went with him.

'Does this remind you of anything?' he asked, as they slid back down the lane on their way home.

'It makes me think of the day we saw how fast we could walk round Queen Street Gardens in the snow,' she replied.

'Do you remember? We tried to get round before our first footprints were lost in the snow.'

Robert laughed. 'That's what I was thinking about too. But I think we're too old for snowballs, don't you?'

Pretending to look shocked, Eliza reminded her brother that he was a minister not a schoolboy!

Just then a snowball flew over his head. It missed, but only just. Although nobody was to be seen anywhere Robert had a sense that perhaps his young friend Geordie was lurking behind the wall. He waved just in case!

When they closed the manse door behind them Eliza told her brother she had a treat for him.

'In ten minutes' time I want you to bring me a bowl of the cleanest snow you can find in the garden. I'll be in the kitchen.'

On cue Robert went out and collected some snow, taking time to look over to Fife and admire the snow-clad hills.

'Now sit down,' his sister said, 'and watch this recipe. It's not like any you've tasted before.'

As Robert was cold he was more than happy to sit in the warmth of the kitchen.

Eliza put flour and beaten eggs into a bowl and mixed them well. Then much to McCheyne's surprise she added some of the snow and mixed it again! More snow was added, then a little more, until the mixture sounded gloopy when she beat it.

'What on earth are you making?' he asked.

Grinning, his sister said he'd know in just a few minutes. The young man watched entranced as she dropped spoonfuls of the mixture on to the girdle.

'Snow pancakes!' he laughed loud and long. 'Who on earth taught you to make them?'

'It's an old Dundee recipe,' Eliza teased. 'Try one.'

Butter dripped off the hot pancake as Robert ate it.

'It's delicious!' he said. 'Absolutely snowily delicious!'

'Now,' said the satisfied cook, 'I've got you in my kitchen and I'm keeping you here until you've heated up… and until we've discussed furnishing this house.'

'I submit,' Robert grinned. 'But don't let's fill the place with grand furniture. It was good of Mum to send chairs and a bed, but she didn't need to buy the most expensive chairs she could find and a huge French bed, did she?'

'She's just trying to make you comfortable,' Eliza said. 'But I agree. Let's furnish it to suit us. After all, it's our home.'

'Hey Minister!'

In the spring of 1837 McCheyne set out on horseback to meet up with his friend Andrew Bonar, who by then was a minister in Perthshire. Tully picked his way up the lane to Perth Road, where they turned left and headed out of town.

'Hey minister!' a familiar voice called.

Robert smiled. 'Hello Geordie! How are you?'

'I'm all right, but I've heard word that there's fever in a close near your church.'

A shiver ran down McCheyne's spine as he thought of the water lying in the back courts, and the sewerage that would not drain away because the ground was soaking after nearly a month of rain.

'I'll be home tomorrow,' the minister told his young friend. 'Come and tell me the news of it then. And you look after yourself. Don't drink from that well beside the pit.'

'I'll not do that, minister,' the lad said. 'I collect rainwater and drink that. In any case, I'm healthy and strong.'

As he road towards Perth Robert couldn't get Geordie out of his mind. He might think he was a strong and healthy specimen but he was small for his twelve years, and painfully thin. For all the world he reminded McCheyne of the young boy whom he'd met in Edinburgh when the Tron Church steeple was burned down.

'I wonder if that poor fellow's still alive and if his master still beats him.'

'How are things in St Peter's?' asked Andrew Bonar when the two friends met. 'Has it ever been as full as it was the night of your induction?'

Relaxing in his friend's company Robert described the last few months. 'The church was built to seat 1175, and 700 people pay seat rents,' he said. 'Though it's a strange tradition paying rent for your church pew!'

Andrew nodded. 'A hundred years from now people will smile at that sort of thing. But we're stuck with it for the time being.'

'Most of that 700 seem to come out on Sundays and more besides. They don't just come from the streets around the church. Some travel from other parts of the city. There are Sundays when I have to push my way into the pulpit through people sitting on the steps because all the seats in the church are taken.'

Bonar decided to tease his friend. 'That's because you never preach for more than 35 minutes. The folk come to hear you so they can be home early for their dinner.'

A blush began somewhere under Robert's collar and crept slowly up his neck. It gave him a healthy looking glow that was in marked contrast to his normally pale skin. 'I can't remember when I last preached for as short a time as that,' he admitted. 'But they listen even though I preach for much longer now. Perhaps they're not so tired as the Carron Ironworkers were, or the miners at Larbert.'

Then, seeing the twinkle in Andrew's eye, Robert burst out laughing.

'I was needing something to cheer me up,' he told his friend when they had both recovered themselves. And he went on to explain about the news he'd heard from Geordie as he rode out of Dundee. But when Robert returned the next day his young informer was smiling. Geordie and Robert had feared cholera but it turned out to be something less serious.

At his ordination Robert was given a gift of a black, silk, preaching-gown. It was such heavy silk that it rustled like a lady's gown as he walked and it embarrassed him no end!

'I don't understand it,' he told his sister. 'I was measured before it was made but there's enough room in it to fit two of me! And it's so grand it feels as though it was made for a bishop at the very least.'

In one of his weekly letters home he said that when he wore his gown he sounded like the leaves of a tree blowing in a gale as he climbed the steps to the pulpit! It's not surprising that he only wore it on Sundays and never at other meetings. As he re-read the letter to his parents, McCheyne thought about his pulpit seat. 'It's the only ornate thing in the church,' he said to himself. 'It's almost like a throne, with its high pointed back and double upholstered arches. In fact, the gown and the pulpit go well together - it's just that I don't fit either a bishop's gown or a throne!'

Had his congregation heard what he was thinking they would have disagreed with their minister. They thought he looked very fine in his preaching-gown, and they were happiest when he was in their pulpit preaching to them. Robert thought he was just an ordinary preacher but his people knew better. McCheyne was one of the most gifted preachers in Scotland. Many of those who came out of interest to hear him speak went away having met with Jesus.

Before Robert had been in Dundee for many months he was invited to be minister of a church in Skirling where the work might have been less hard and the conditions better for him. Robert was not at all tempted to move as he knew God had called him to Dundee. Mrs McCheyne had other ideas and wrote to her son telling him what a good move it would be and how his health would benefit from the fresh country air.

'Dear Mother,' he wrote in reply to her letter, 'you must just make up your mind to let me be murdered among the lanes of Dundee instead of seeing me fattening on the green grass of Skirling. Perhaps moving there would be good for my frail body, but if I'd gone I think my soul would have turned sickly and that most precious part of me would have withered.'

Robert was in Dundee and he felt he should stay there.

A year after McCheyne and his sister moved to the city they were walking together along Perth Road early one Thursday evening.

'Hello Geordie!' said Robert, when he saw his young friend at the bottom of St Peter's Street. 'What are you doing out at this time of night?'

The lad shrugged his shoulders.

'I was just wondering the same about you. I thought church was only for Sundays but it's Thursday night and the place looks full. In fact, there's something on here nearly every night.'

Knowing he had plenty of time Robert suggested that Eliza go in ahead of him. He would follow in a few minutes.

'It's like this,' the minister explained. 'The elders decided that they would like a prayer meeting in the middle of the week as well as the three Sunday services.'

'What do you do at a prayer meeting?' was the puzzled response.

'We sing, read the Bible and I preach a short sermon.'

'That's just the same as a service,' Geordie interrupted.

'How would you know?' Robert asked gently. 'You're never in church.'

The lad scratched the back of his left leg with his right bare foot.

'I don't need to be in church to hear you; I listen from outside.' Embarrassed by the admission, he went on. 'So what's different about a prayer meeting then?'

Robert explained that many of the men prayed aloud during the meeting, that it wasn't only the minister who prayed.'

'I see,' said Geordie as he slunk into the shadows. 'You get other folk to do your work for you.'

During his sermon that evening Robert wondered if, as well as the 800 people in church, there was a cold, barefooted, undersized teenager listening outside. During a time of silent prayer he asked God to bless young Geordie.

'I don't know any other job that keeps a man busy morning, afternoon and evening,' Eliza said, as she laid her brother's lunch on the table. 'And don't blame me if this isn't as tasty as usual. It's been over boiling water to keep it hot for an hour because you're so late home.'

Realising that his normally placid sister was feeling more than a little stressed he suggested that they took a walk after lunch before he went out to do his afternoon visiting.

'I'm sorry,' he said, as they set off down Strawberry Bank towards the River Tay. 'There's so much to do that I sometimes forget the time. Take this morning, for example. I was in my study preparing for the Bible Class this evening when a message came saying that old Mrs Baxter was dying. She was alone apart from a neighbour and I didn't feel I could leave her until she had passed away. I've got visits I have to do this afternoon and then there are the young folk this evening.'

Eliza was silent. 'I didn't know that's what happened this morning,' she said. 'I'm sorry I was so grumpy. It's just that I worry about you. Sometimes you're out visiting sick people who are healthier than you are. Robert, you look so thin and pale.'

By then they were standing by a fence at the riverside. Having a quick look around to make sure they were not being seen, McCheyne put his hands on the top rail and did a gate vault over to the other side.

'I may be pale. I may be skinny,' he told his sister. 'But I can still do things you can't do!'

Eliza looked down at her wide full-length dress and laughed aloud.

'If we women didn't have to wear such ridiculous clothes I'd join you in the fun!'

As they turned and walked back they saw several little boats on the Tay and the ferry leaving for Fife.

'What a busy place this is,' Eliza smiled. 'I suppose your business means you fit in well in Dundee.'

That night before he went to bed Robert wrote a letter to his brother. Willie was still at home with their parents in Edinburgh.

'There were about 250 young people at the Bible Class tonight. I taught them by what I call the geographical method. I drew a sketch of the Sea of Galilee on the board then had them looking up the Bible verses that mention it. We went through the stories one by one; with me showing where we think each of them happened. Now they have a mental picture of where Jesus called his fishermen disciples, where he stilled the storm and where he healed the mad man among the tombs. I think that kind of teaching helps things to become real. By the way,' he added before signing his name, 'I'm enclosing a sketch of the Sea of Galilee like the one I used tonight. Don't laugh at it. I try my best!'

As he relaxed before falling asleep that night McCheyne tried to imagine the Holy Land. Was his mental picture of the Sea of Galilee really what it looked like? he wondered. Rolling over on to his side he closed his eyes with the thought that he'd never know because that was one place he would never be. His home was Dundee. His people were the people of Dundee. And with the beginnings of tuberculosis already diagnosed there was no saying how long or short a time he had to tell them about Jesus. Any thought of travelling abroad was out of the question.

Next door to St Peter's was a school run by the church. Children attended classes during the day and there were evening classes for girls who worked in factories or were servants in the big houses. Although McCheyne thought it was important that the children and young people learned to read and write, he believed it was even more important that they learned about the Lord Jesus and trusted in him as their Saviour. He often sat by the bedside of those who were dying, many of them young people, and not all of them were Christians. It broke his heart when an unbeliever died. But while he was sad when a Christian died, he had the comfort of knowing they were now with Jesus. Often Robert thought about his brother David, and about the glow on his face just as he died. He knew David had said his goodbyes and had been looking forward to being in heaven.

'Good evening, Sadie,' Robert said to a teenager as she went up St Peter's Street on her way to the evening class. 'How has your day been?'

Sadie rubbed her eyes with her sleeve. 'It's not been the best, Mr McCheyne,' she admitted. 'There was an accident in the mill and it was horrible to see.'

'Do you want to tell me about it?' he asked.

She shook her head and made to walk on up the side of the churchyard. Then she hesitated and turned round. Robert had waited in case she changed her mind. He walked up the hill with the girl and they sat down on the wall at the top. It was light enough for the minister to see tear streaks on her face. They'd been left to dry because she couldn't stop work long enough to wipe her tears away without getting a row for slacking, and she'd come straight from her work to the evening class.

'I work with a weaver and stand beside his loom to see when threads break. When one does break I dive under the loom, grab both loose ends and tie them together quickly so that he doesn't have to stop the loom. Stopping the loom costs money because it breaks the weaver's rhythm and it takes him time to get it back up to speed again.'

Robert pictured the scene, and it wasn't a nice one. He knew that underneath the looms where girls like Sadie worked the factory floor was thick with fine dust that clogged their lungs as well as irritating their eyes and making them cough. It was so bad that most of the girls wore a cloth wrapped round their face to cover their nose and mouth.

Sadie continued, 'Well, Martha Morrison works on the loom next to me. She's younger than I am and not so fast. Martha's threads kept breaking this morning. She had four or five, one after the other and she was slowing down. The weaver kicked her under the loom to hurry her on. Martha got such a fright she jumped and her hair caught in the loom.'

Sadie's face crumpled and she struggled against tears. But she swallowed hard and went on with the story. Robert realised that she was seeing in her mind's eye what had happened. 'Martha was dragged along underneath before the weaver knew what was happening. By the time he'd stopped the loom....'

The girl was unable to go on.

'Is she badly injured?' Robert asked gently.

Nodding slowly Sadie said quietly, 'She was scalped, Mr McCheyne.'

Robert felt sick, and he couldn't begin to imagine what Sadie felt having seen it.

'Let's go into the vestry and pray,' he suggested. 'I don't think you're fit for classes this evening.'

The following morning the news went round the area like wildfire. Young Martha Morrison was dead and the factory owner was looking for a girl to take her place. Although everyone knew the dangers of the job there was a queue of mothers with daughters at the mill already. They were so desperate for the money that they had to take the risk.

'I can't bear thinking about that poor child,' Eliza said, as she and her brother ate their evening meal. 'And it breaks my heart that even before she's buried another little girl is crawling under her loom.'

Robert put down his teacup. The thought wounded him as much as it did his sister.

'Are their homes really so poor that children of six have to work in these terrible conditions?'

'Yes, they are. Though sometimes it makes me angry rather than sad,' McCheyne sighed.

Eliza looked puzzled. 'What do you mean?'

'If you were to walk along the alleyways at a time of night when no decent woman should be out you'd know exactly what I mean. There are men there who have earned enough money to keep their children from starving, but instead of taking it home to their hard-working and broken-hearted wives, they take it to the beer shop. There they sit, drinking their children's food away and they end up snoring on the floor out of their minds with drink. Some of them smoke till they can't speak for coughing when you'd think they'd have enough dirt in their lungs from Dundee's smoke-filled air. And if they have enough of their senses left they spend what's remaining of their money on gambling.'

Robert closed his eyes. It wasn't often that he spoke so graphically to his sister of things that really hurt. But his defences were right down at the thought of the little child who'd just started Martha Morrison's job.

'What can we do to help?' the practical Eliza asked.

'We have collections for the poor already,' answered McCheyne. 'And I make sure it goes where it's most needed. But however much the congregation gives, there are always more people needing help. The only thing that will change the situation is for those desperate men to come to Christ. The Lord is the only one who can make a difference in this dark city.'

And the Lord had begun to make a difference. Right from the beginning of Robert's ministry men, women and young people were being converted, sometimes in ones and twos, sometimes in larger numbers. When he arrived home with eyes shining with joy his sister knew that another soul had been saved. But always there was a burden on Robert's heart that kept him praying for more. Had every person in St Peter's become a Christian he would still have longed and prayed for more conversions. He was not a greedy man, he just loved the Lord Jesus and longed with all his heart that others would love him too. That gave a fire to his preaching that made its mark on people's hearts. He became so well known that there were very few people in Dundee who didn't know the name Robert Murray McCheyne.

'I'm slowing dying of tuberculosis,' he thought over and over again. 'And there are thousands of people out there who are dying of sin. I must tell as many as I can where they can find forgiveness. And I must do it as soon as I can for I don't know how long I've got to live, and I don't know how long they've got either.'

Crash Landing!

'Happy birthday!' Eliza said, when her brother opened the dining-room door on the morning of 21st May 1838. 'How does it feel to have reached your quarter century?'

'You should know!' laughed Robert. 'You got there first!'

'Thank you for that reminder of my great age,' the young woman teased. 'I've a good mind not to give you your present.'

But it didn't stop her giving it, and the birthday boy was delighted with his new book.

'Now that you are 25, are you going to grow up?' Eliza asked as they drank their breakfast tea.

Robert shook his head. 'I don't think so. I'll wait a while yet.'

Three months later McCheyne demonstrated that he was still a boy at heart. One weekend he was staying with a family as he preached in the nearby church. One of the boys there was quite an active child. Robert showed him all sorts of gymnastic exercises and the pair had a splendid time.

'What you really need is a bar to exercise on,' he said to the boy. 'I'll tell you exactly how it should be built. You want two upright posts just over a metre apart. One should be nailed to that tree there. Do you understand?'

The boy nodded enthusiastically. He understood all

right; and he understood this could be great fun!

'Now,' said Robert, 'both posts should have a series of circular holes cut in them so a bar can be put between them at whatever height you want. I'll draw you a picture of it.'

The pair flopped to the ground under the tree and the picture was duly drawn. When Robert left to go home nothing would do but that the gymnastic apparatus should be built. On his next visit to his friends McCheyne was delighted to find the bars built exactly to his specifications.

'Is it strong enough to take my weight?' he asked.

He was assured that a heavier man had tried it out and both the apparatus and the man had survived. Robert sprang at the bar and hung by his heels and hands six feet off the ground ready to swing up and somersault off... when one of the upright poles split at its lowest hole and the thing crashed to the ground with Robert in an unconscious heap on top of it. A doctor was sent for but no serious injury was found. Battered and bruised, he stayed on for a couple of days before setting out for Dundee. His original plan was to travel back home with his friend Mr Guthrie.

'My dear Eliza,' he wrote to his sister. 'You will be surprised that I've not come with Mr Guthrie but I had a tumble and it's thought best that I stay here another day. He will explain what happened. Don't worry about me. The doctor says that I've done no lasting damage!'

But it was something more serious than a sports injury that bothered McCheyne later that year. His cough wouldn't go away and the strain caused his heart to beat violently. He was often weary beyond words. Eliza, desperately worried, insisted that he see the doctor.

'Sit down,' the doctor ordered Robert, after he had examined him. 'Listen to me. If you want to recover you must take several months of complete rest. And I can't be responsible for the consequences if you don't.'

What the doctor didn't realise was that his patient knew that he probably would not live to be old. What mattered to Robert Murray McCheyne was that he did the Lord's work as long as he lived. The young minister's care of his people meant more to him than his care of himself. Nothing the folk of Dundee needed was too much trouble for him, and the door of his house at Strawberry Bank was open day and night to anyone in need.

Having done some plain speaking, the doctor smiled at the young man and told him that he wouldn't charge for his visit. Rather than argue Robert waited until later before putting his goose quill pen to paper in a mixture of English and Latin, and sending the poem and the fee to his doctor.

On receiving it the doctor smiled and shook his head as he read it to his wife.

Dear Doctor, allow me to borrow a leaf
From your book of prescriptions, commanding and brief,
'Hoc aurum et papyr.' Mix - pocket call 'Dust'!
And swallow it quickly. Come, Doctor, you must.
I had sooner want stipend, want dinner, want tea,
Than my doctor should ever work wanting his fee.
Forgive this intrusion; and let me remain,
In haste, your affectionate, R M McCheyne.

Over the days that followed Robert's heart problem became more acute, to the point that he was seriously ill, and it was decided that he should go with Eliza back to

Edinburgh for a break. Edinburgh doctors confirmed the advice he was given in Dundee. The young man needed complete rest and his family was there to make sure he took it. Letters began arriving from the people of St Peter's, and if their minister had ever doubted their affection these must have reassured him. By the end of January he felt able to write to his congregation telling them how he longed to be back among them but was still too unwell. A month later he wrote again reminding them of what he had taught them, and that he had been so passionate that he sometimes preached with tears running down his face.

Resting for a moment before finishing the letter, Robert's heart felt full at the thought of Dundee. 'Will I ever see them again?' he wondered. Then with a slow, tired hand he concluded the letter.

'Is this my final farewell?' Robert asked himself. 'If it is I leave these dear people safe in God's hands.'

While the folk of Dundee were precious to their minister they were not his only concern. For years Robert had been interested in Jewish people. He felt sure that although they had rejected Jesus, their promised Messiah, God had not abandoned them and that they still had a special place in his plans. Robert was not the only one who believed that was what the Bible said. Several of his friends thought the same, and it was a subject much talked about when they went to visit their sick colleague. The Church of Scotland had formed a committee to discuss the matter and it was decided to send a delegation to Europe and Palestine 'to collect information respecting the Jews, their number, condition and character.' But who would go? Eventually it was agreed to send four men: Dr Alexander Black, Dr Alexander Keith, Robert Woodrow and McCheyne's good friend, Andrew Bonar.

'Do you think there's any possibility of Robert going with them?' one leading churchman asked.

'He'd be ideal for the job,' the other replied. 'But don't you think it might kill him?'

'Actually I think it might do him good. The warm weather and change could bring him back to health.'

In the event Mr Woodrow had to drop out for health reasons and the very unhealthy Robert Murray McCheyne took his place!

The people of St Peter's were shattered. They wanted their minister well again and back among them. They missed seeing him in the street with the local children and hearing him in the pulpit. Young and old alike were disappointed at this turn of events. But before Robert was due to set out on his great adventure a letter arrived from the elders of St Peter's that set his heart at rest. It assured him that they understood that God had work for him to do and that it wasn't limited to Dundee.

'May the God of all grace... be the companion of your journey,' the letter said, as it drew to its close. 'May he refresh your soul by his love. May he take you safely to the place of your destination. There may God command blessing upon you.'

With his congregations's blessing Robert arranged for William C Burns to look after St Peter's, then he began to get organised for his journey. Burns had just finished his studies and one of the last things McCheyne did before leaving was to write to his young locum.

'I hope you may be a thousand times more blessed among them than I ever was. Perhaps there are many souls that would never have been saved under my ministry, who may be touched under yours.'

Robert wasn't the only one writing letters. On 27th March 1839, when he left for London he had a letter in his pocket from his father.

'Seeing so many people and speaking so much will bring back your complaints, can't you take things more coolly?'

By the time Robert was 25 years old you would have thought his father would have known that such advice would fall on deaf ears!

The travelling companions met in London a few days later, and after a farewell service on 9th April they headed to the south coast of England and Robert's first trip abroad.

'Raise the anchor!' the mate cried, when all his crew and passengers were aboard.

There was a rattling and a clanking of metal chains then two sailors hauled the anchor on deck and the ship began to ease away from the quay at Dover. Sailors swarmed everywhere, some up the mast, others pulling ropes here, there and everywhere.

'It's fascinating watching them,' Andrew Bonar said.

Robert agreed. 'You'd think all these coils of rope would get into tangles that could never be undone.'

His friend laughed. 'If that happened we'd all end up at the bottom of the sea.'

'Look!' they both said at once, pointing in opposite directions. McCheyne won the round and pointed to the chalk cliffs of Dover. 'They're very impressive,' he commented, 'I wonder how deep the cliffs go underwater. And look at the castle up there.' He pointed to the top of the cliff. 'No invading army could get into Dover without being seen from that vantage point.'

Robert turned to see what his friend had seen, expecting it to be another ship. He was wrong. Andrew had seen the French coast.

'I didn't realise you could see France from England,' said Robert. 'But I suppose it's only about 20 miles away.'

'But quite a rough 20 miles,' Andrew grimaced. 'And I'm not a good sailor.'

The English Channel was boisterous and Bonar's stomach was first to feel the effect of it. He was not sorry when the ship berthed at Boulogne after three hours at sea.

The next leg of their travels took them through France to Paris then south to Dijon then Marseilles. On either side of them were plantations of low, gnarled trees.

'I suppose those are vines,' commented Dr Black. 'Somehow I thought they would be taller than that.'

'Oui, monsieur,' a French fellow traveller said. He understood enough English to know what had been said. 'They are old, very old. Some say the vines are a thousand years old, maybe two thousand.' He then asked where they were going. 'Ahh!' he sighed deeply. 'Where you are going you will see vines much more impressive than these.'

'In what way?' Robert asked.

'In Palestine you may see the same vines as Jesus saw with his own two eyes.'

'Do you think he was right?' wondered Andrew, when the four friends were alone.

Dr Keith nodded his head. 'I've heard they can live for an amazing time. So perhaps we will.'

But vines were not on Robert's mind that night as he settled to sleep. 'I wonder if the Sea of Galilee is just as I described it to the young people in Dundee or if I got it wildly wrong.'

From Italy McCheyne wrote to Eliza about the food. 'Meals here begin with different kinds of fish, then eggs dressed in various ways, then mutton, beef, chicken … young peas and new potatoes, oranges, figs, nuts and fruits of all kinds. The only thing to drink is wine. How happy I will be to get back to simple food again! Oh, by the way, the Palace of Genoa was brilliant!'

Another letter was sent to Edinburgh, this time from Alexandria to Robert's parents.

'You cannot imagine what this city harbour is like! It baffles description: boys with donkeys, men with camels, wild-looking porters, Greeks and Turks, all roaring in Arabic, all eager to be at us and our luggage!'

'I think we should go to the Synagogue today,' said Dr Black.

They all agreed that would be a good idea. When they arrived outside the synagogue they were guided up a dark stair and through a long poorly lit passage into a room.

'There are just ten men here,' Andrew counted. 'From their clothes I guess these three are from Egypt, but the others seem to come from elsewhere.'

As they watched the service the visitors thought the Jewish men didn't seem to be very interested in what was going on apart from when they pulled their prayer shawls over their mouths and prayed quietly.

Robert found himself thinking about their tasselled prayer shawls. 'They are very precious to the men,' he remembered.

'When he's 13 years old a Jewish boy becomes a man at a ceremony called his Bar Mitzvah. He's given his prayer shawl then and he uses it for the rest of his life before being buried in it. The blue and white tassels each have five knots in them to symbolise the five books of the Law of Moses.'

As soon as the service was over the Jewish men spoke to their visitors, opening up the ark in which they kept their sacred books and showing them their copies of the Law. The Scots spoke to the men about the Messiah for whom they were waiting, and explained that Jesus is the Messiah, and that he has already come.

The following day, 15th May 1839, the travellers prepared for the next leg of their journey - across the desert.

'What a place this is!' grinned Robert, as they strolled through the bazaar. 'They have everything... but what do we actually need?'

'Rugs to sleep on,' Andrew said, 'and we'll each require a blanket. And two tents, of course. We don't really want to sleep in the open air.'

'Anything else?' his friend asked.

Bonar laughed. 'A lot! And if you would stop admiring the bracelets you could take back to Eliza you'd remember that we need to find a guide, a cook, cooking utensils, cutlery and dishes... not to mention some food!'

McCheyne left the jewellery stall and got back to work. By the end of the morning they had everything they needed including Ibraim and Ahmel, their guide and cook. By evening Ibraim had them all in order and had told the Scots that they would have to be up and off early the next morning.

'What's that?' gulped Robert, in what seemed the

middle of the night.

Andrew sat bolt upright. 'It's Ibraim! What do you think he wants at this hour?'

They listened to the racket outside. There seemed to be a whole herd of donkeys, each with a driver shouting at the top of his voice!

'We need to go now, sirs! It's time to go!'

Bonar swallowed hard, then called out more kindly than he felt that it was not time to go, it was time to sleep, and that they would leave at 7 o'clock. When the four still sleepy Scots eventually appeared they found 16 donkeys waiting patiently and their 16 drivers waiting very impatiently!

'What a sight!' Dr Keith said, as they left Alexandria. 'There are the donkeys and drivers, ourselves with Ibraim and Ahmel, and ten Egyptian lads running at our side with our luggage. And I've heard that two more donkeys are joining us.'

Travelling in the desert was a new experience for the four men and they found it fascinating.

'What's the white crusty stuff on the sand?' Robert asked Ibraim.

Their guide picked some up and gave it to him.

'This used to be a salt lake,' he explained. 'Its water has been dried up by the sun leaving just salt.'

McCheyne licked his hand. 'So it is!' he said. 'Pure salt.'

It was Andrew Bonar who noticed the pool of water first. 'Over there!' he said, pointing left. 'Can't you see it?'

They did. But although it looked very real in the distance they were assured that the pool was a mirage. The first real water they saw was the River Nile, and from there they headed north to the Mediterranean Sea. But not all their travelling was done by day.

'Owing to the restless impatience of our guides and servants we were obliged to strike our tents at midnight,' Andrew Bonar recorded. 'The moon was nearly full and the sky was cloudless as we travelled for some hours through the countryside. Sometimes we came upon Arab huts made of palm branches and were met by the angry growling of their dogs. Arriving at the sea we rode along the shore, the waves frequently washing the donkeys' feet. What problems we had stopping ourselves from falling asleep and we didn't always manage it. The men and boys with us were very amused when we dozed and fell off our donkeys on to the wet sand! To crown it all there were frequent flashes of lightning to awaken us during our night ride.'

Dr Black, Dr Keith, Andrew and Robert were adventurers and they were certainly having an adventure!

Journey of Discovery

The four Scotsmen hardly had time to become used to riding on donkeys when a new form of transport became necessary. On 24th May they went a short walk from their tents and when they returned eight camels awaited them! They watched the creatures being loaded. Robert took in every detail in order to tell Eliza when he saw her again.

'At one word of command the animal sinks down to the sand with its limbs crouched under it. A wooden frame is fastened to the highest part of its back and a network of ropes is attached to it. I think this is used to secure luggage. A carpet and covering are placed right on top to form a soft saddle and the rider sits either astride it or sideways. There is no stirrup or bridle and balancing is going to take a bit of getting used to. While this whole operation is taking place the camel moans sadly and he sometimes tries to bite!'

Andrew Bonar watched his friend's first antics on his camel. 'Wait till the camel is down and still,' Robert was told. He waited. 'Now mount and let him rise slowly. You'll feel you're falling backwards when he gets up on his front legs and as if you're falling forwards when he stands upright. Balance your own weight to stop yourself falling off.'

Robert mounted the camel and struggled to balance as the camel rose to its feet.

'Don't worry!' Ibraim shouted. 'Nobody ever hurts himself falling off a camel.'

That didn't prove to be the case. A few days later Dr Black fell from his mount and the others slipped from their beasts and ran to help him. He was in a state of semi-consciousness. To shade him from the burning sun, the Arabs pitched a tent, sprinkled some of their precious water over it and laid the poor man inside to rest and recover. They were glad the next day was Sunday.

Thirteen days after leaving Alexandria the men woke early, very excited at what the day held for them. They were mounted by 4 am, and travelled at first by moonlight. By five they had reached the head of the valley and started to climb up a mountain pass. As the sun rose and began to heat the air the scent of the wild flowers was glorious. It was daylight when they reached the top of the pass where they rested to enjoy the views in both directions.

'What's growing in that plantation?' Robert asked, as they picked their way down the other side.

'Those are olive trees,' Ibraim said. 'This is a good place for olives. The next village we come to is called Karieh, and it's famous for its olives. Pomegranates and figs grow there too. They are in blossom at this time of year.'

The Scotsmen could hardly take in the beauty of their surroundings when they reached Karieh. The trees were like soapsuds of blossom and sleek black-haired goats grazed between them. Through the village and down the valley they went before starting climbing yet again.

'Every pass takes us nearer Jerusalem,' Andrew commented to his friend. 'But there do seem to be a lot of them!'

At last they neared the final summit, seven hours after starting out. Robert slid off his camel.

'Where are you going?' asked Dr Black.

McCheyne grinned. 'This creature can only travel at 3 miles an hour and I can run faster than that. I'm off to see Jerusalem!'

Dr Black laughed, and remembered what it felt like to be 25 years old.

Running ahead of his fellow travellers, Robert reached the summit and stood transfixed.

'I can see Jerusalem,' he whispered.

The camel train stopped and the other travellers dismounted. Silently they stood together looking into the far distance. Each was lost in his own thoughts.

'Jerusalem, the Holy City,' thought Dr Black.

Andrew sighed. 'Jesus knew this view. He saw what I'm seeing.'

'That's where my Lord Jesus died,' said Dr Keith to himself, his heart overwhelmed with a mixture of feelings.

Robert shook his head disbelievingly. 'I can hardly believe this is real.'

Setting out again they moved towards the city they had seen so often in their imaginations and had never expected to see in reality.

Andrew Bonar recorded their first impressions.

'The feelings of that hour could not even be spoken. We moved forward almost in silence. While passing along the pathway immediately under the western wall and entering the Jaffa Gate we could understand the Bible's words and we made them our own. "Is this the city which men call the perfection of beauty, the joy of the whole earth." Its dark walls, and the glance we got of slippery narrow streets, with low badly built houses and poor people, suggested nothing of the magnificence of former days. But we were soon to learn that all the elements of Jerusalem's glory and beauty are still remaining in its wonderful situation.'

Investigating the city of Jerusalem was something the Scotsmen would always remember. They saw the Mount of Olives and the road along which Jesus walked to be crucified. The people were interesting too, and fascinated by the quaint strangers. The British Consul introduced the ministers to Mr Nicolayson, a missionary who was able to give them the information they needed.

'About 10,000 Jewish people live in the city,' they were told. 'Most of them are from Central Europe and Spain. As a rule they are very strict in their religion. Many have been so badly treated by Christians in the past that they are fearful of us, and a number would go as far as hating what we stand for.'

Robert listened sadly. He knew that some people had called the Jewish people Christ-killers and that saddened him terribly. 'Christ died for my sins,' he thought. 'I'm as guilty as any Jew of the death of the Lord Jesus.'

For five hours Mr Nicolayson talked with the men who took notes of what he said and of what they saw around them. The highlight of their time there was when the missionary took them to an upper room, much like the one in which Jesus took his last supper, and the men followed their Lord in word and action in a simple Communion service. Before leaving the Holy City the delegation noted the result of their investigations.

'I think we have to report four things about the Jewish people in Jerusalem,' said Dr Black. 'First, they are superstitions in the extreme. Second, missionaries would have few points of contact with the Jews and any missionary activity would have to be done on a one-to-one basis. Third, here it is regarded as an awful calamity for a Jew to become a Christian. Fourth, the Jewish people in the Holy Land are dependent on money coming from their fellow Jews in Europe. And if anyone here shows an interest in the Lord his money is immediately cut off.'

Andrew nodded his head. 'I think that sums up the situation exactly.'

The fact that McCheyne spent hours most days travelling didn't stop him writing letters. Family and friends heard news of his travels.

'Since I last wrote to you,' he told a friend, 'we have never slept in beds. We spread our mats on the sand and God watches over us when we are under the cover of our frail tents. We often hear the cry of the wolves at night and there are many lynxes and hyenas in this mountain. But God keeps us safe. The burning heat of the desert, the long tiring journeys - sometimes 12 to 14 hours a day on a camel - the insatiable thirst and our weakness are all very trying.'

The touring party set off by boat to Beirut but by the time they arrived there Dr Keith was very unwell and it was decided that he and Dr Black should return home early to Scotland.

'There is a converted Jew living in Beirut,' Andrew and Robert were told. 'Would you like to meet him?'

Of course they would!

Erasmus was just the man they needed. Not only was he a Jew and a Christian but he knew the situation in Palestine like the back of his hand and he spoke Arabic, Polish, German and English as well as Hebrew!

'Would you like me to accompany you on your journey?' Erasmus asked the two friends.

Bonar and McCheyne were pleased to accept that kind offer, seeing it as a gift from God. One of the first places they went was the Sea of Galilee and Robert was delighted to discover that he had not been teaching his Bible Class pupils nonsense!

What had been a wonderful trip turned into a nightmare for Andrew when his friend took ill on board a ship between Cyprus and Smyrna, so ill that he lapsed into unconsciousness. When Robert regained consciousness he was so unwell that he was sure he would die. But with careful nursing in Smyrna he regained strength enough to go on. At a time when travelling was far from easy the men went from Smyrna through the Bosphorus and across the Black Sea towards the River Danube.

'We'll try to visit all the Jewish communities on the way home,' Bonar explained to an elderly Englishman they met on their way.

'Are you travelling direct?' asked the man.

Andrew grinned. 'Not exactly,' he admitted, 'we hope to go by Moldavia, Romania then Austrian and Prussian Poland.'

'How long will that take?'

'We've left ourselves two-and-a-half months to get back to Scotland.'

'I see your friend taking notes everywhere he goes,' the man said. 'He's a studious fellow.'

Andrew smiled. 'That's true,' he agreed. 'But he's not always working.'

The Englishman raised his eyebrows in puzzlement.

'Robert!' Bonar called. 'Would you mind showing this gentleman some of your sketches?'

For the half-hour that followed McCheyne leafed through his sketchbook showing drawing after drawing of the places they had visited. There were sketches of Jerusalem, the Mount of Olives and the Sea of Galilee. And of course there were sketches of camels. Even looking at them made Andrew's stomach heave. As they worked their way through the sketchbook Robert wove Bible stories into the pictures is such a way that his new friend didn't realise he was hearing a sermon! It was only when they finished their artistic tour that the thought occurred to him.

'You must be a persuasive preacher,' the Englishman said. 'You almost make me want to believe.'

McCheyne looked earnest. 'It's a matter of life and death, you know. When the Day of Judgment dawns God will not be impressed by those who say they didn't trust in Jesus because they just didn't get around to it.'

The older man rose to leave the room. 'That's a sobering thought,' he said, as he closed the door behind him.

Andrew Bonar and Robert Murray McCheyne were not only interested in visiting synagogues. When they had the opportunity they went into schools too. On one occasion they were made more welcome by the pupils than their teacher.

'As we entered a classroom in one school,' Robert told someone he met later, 'the teacher was in the act of applying a bastinado to a boy. The other boys shouted out for us to help their friend. A bastinado is a twisted rope fixed on a short stick round the feet of the culprit, who is laid on the floor on his face. Then a strong whip made of ox hide is applied to the soles of his feet! When he saw us the teacher

107

released the boy. I'm glad we arrived when we did and I'm quite sure the child was too. We bought a whip and a bastinado as souvenirs.'

'Would you like to attend a Jewish wedding?' the men were asked at Jassy in Moldavia.

Andrew and Robert looked at each other and nodded.

'That's very kind of you,' McCheyne said. 'Thank you.'

They arrived at the arranged time only to find that there was to be a long delay.

'The bridegroom didn't bring the customary string of diamonds for the girl's head-dress,' they were told. 'He has gone to find the money to buy one. Go away and come back later.'

But when they returned the wedding was over. Their host described the day's events.

'Early in the morning a poet went to the bride's house and told her to cry for forgiveness. She and her maids would have been in tears during the talk that lasted over an hour. The poet then did the same at the groom's house. A band of musicians brought the groom to the synagogue then went for the bride. They stood under a canopy on four poles for the ceremony. Seven blessings were said over a cup of wine, the ring was then put on the bride's finger before a final seven blessings on the wine. After that the goblet of wine was smashed on the floor. The married couple then went to the bride's house and we'll find them there.'

'I must remember to draw the bride's dress to show Eliza,' thought Robert, as they walked along the road.

Before leaving Moldavia they wrote a report for the Church of Scotland.

'1. In the cities of Moldavia and Wallachia there are between 25,000 and 31,000 Jews. 2. The Jews here seem more open-minded than in Jerusalem. 3. Missionaries might not meet too much opposition. 4. Because Jews here have jobs their support cannot be withheld if they show an interest in Jesus. 5. Those who become Christians here might take the good news to their fellow Jews in places where missionaries would not be welcome.'

A letter Robert wrote from Poland must have caused some concern back home in Scotland.

'I had a narrow escape from two evil-minded shepherds. They made signs that I should go with them. I refused. Then they showed me that I must. I persisted in saying I would not. Not to be outdone they threw themselves on the ground in front of me! I pushed them aside and ran. Although I could easily have outrun them I didn't want to start my heart pounding. So I stopped, and with my trusty walking stick stood to defend myself. But as I couldn't bring myself to hit them they soon closed in on me, and it ended as a wrestling match in which my coat was torn from top to bottom. I was so tired I could do nothing but lie down on the ground and rest. I don't know what they made of that because they just turned round and left! I heard later that they probably meant to rob me and that they might easily have used a knife to keep me quiet. It was God who looked after me that day. I've such a lot to thank him for!'

There was more to Poland than evil-minded shepherds as the travellers found out. That country had the largest Jewish community in Europe; they were even mistaken for Jews themselves!

'You will report to the Commissary of Police,' Robert and Andrew were ordered early in the morning of 4th October.

Wondering what the matter was they went to the police station.

'Why are you Jews travelling under false passports?' the Officer asked roughly, as he took away their documents.

The men explained that they were not Jewish and that their passports were quite in order. The Officer produced a letter that showed McCheyne and Bonar had been attending synagogue services! It took some time to convince him that they were Scottish Christian ministers and that the Jewish things they had with them were mementos of their travels. Eventually their passports were returned to them and they were free to leave.

Later Robert and Andrew talked long into the night. Their subject was anti-Semitism, hatred of the Jews.

'I suppose there have been those who have hated the Jewish people since the day Christ was crucified,' Andrew said, stifling a yawn. It was bed-time, but they had reached the stage where it is less effort to continue talking than to change into nightclothes.

Robert shook his head. 'It goes back beyond that. When you read the Old Testament you see them being oppressed hundreds of years before the Lord was born. They were God's chosen people and they weren't afraid to tell that to the nations around them. Imagine how that made their enemies feel!'

Struggling to stay awake Andrew tried to engage his imagination. 'I see what you mean,' he said. 'The Jewish people were proud of being chosen and that would make others feel very inferior, especially at those times in their history when God was obviously on their side.'

McCheyne had passed sleepiness and his mind was now in overdrive.

'Christ's crucifixion was one more thing to accuse them of,' he insisted. 'It wasn't the cause of anti-Semitism, just another reason to continue it.'

They talked through the history of the Jews so far as they knew it, tracing their spread throughout Europe and into Britain.

'Part of the problem in European cities and in Britain is that when Jewish people arrive they go where their fellow Jews are, and their communities grow but remain in the same areas. They become almost towns within cities, with their own shops, factories, schools, and their own language. The people who live in neighbouring areas sometimes feel threatened by them just because they neither know Jewish people nor understand their culture.'

By the time Robert had finished what he had to say his friend was asleep in his chair. Robert smiled as he wakened Andrew to tell him it was time to go to sleep!

An End and a New Beginning

Eventually Bonar and McCheyne arrived in Hamburg, the last major city they were to visit before returning home. Their investigations began much as usual with visits to synagogues and schools. Then on 29th October an extraordinary thing happened.

'I thought you might like to read this,' a friend said, handing them a British newspaper.

Robert read the report to which the man was pointing. Then he read it again, his eyes gleaming. Handing it to Andrew without a word, he waited for his reaction.

'Revivals in Kilsyth and Dundee,' he whispered. 'Dundee,' repeated Robert. 'I wonder...'

'You mean you've not heard about this?' queried their friend, 'I thought you'd be able to tell me what it was all about.'

Shaking his head, McCheyne explained that their mail hadn't caught up with them and this was the first they'd heard about it.

Having read the article again, Andrew commented that it really said very little. 'But Dundee is mentioned.'

The two young men were delighted as well as curious as they discussed what might have happened. Had hundreds of people been converted all at once? Had many Christians had their faith deepened? Were children and young people involved? They had plenty of questions but no answers. With their Jewish investigations over they could hardly wait to

113

get back to Scotland to find out all about it. Leaving Hamburg for Sholau just after midnight on Monday 4th November, after a truly appalling voyage they berthed in London three days later. When they arrived back they heard that Dr Black and Dr Keith, who had both been very unwell, were still recuperating in Budapest!

Robert returned to Dundee on 23rd November, having been away from his congregation for almost a year. What a welcome awaited him! It was as though the souls of his congregation were on fire for the Lord.

'Start right at the beginning and tell me what happened,' McCheyne urged William Burns. 'And take your time.'

William thought back over the months he had served as locum minister in St Peter's and worked out where to start his story.

'When I first came here people listened very carefully to my sermons and some became Christians, just as happened with your preaching before you went away. Young people seemed especially interested. Then in July my father asked me to preach at his Communion in Kilsyth. I ended up staying three weeks because the Holy Spirit came in revival. Strong men and women wept over their sins; children did too. And a great many people were converted. Christians were also affected, seeing anew the holiness of God. It was as though the rushing wind of Pentecost had fallen on the town.'

Robert said nothing; he didn't want to interrupt the story he was hearing.

'I returned to Dundee on 8th August,' William continued, 'and at the end of the next service I took I told the people what had happened in Kilsyth. Almost 100 people waited behind because they felt the need of the Holy Spirit's blessing. The following evening the church was full to overflowing for the prayer meeting and it was like Kilsyth all over again. People were weeping over their sins; some cried aloud for God's mercy. From then on there were prayer meetings every night and revival swept through St Peter's.'

'That must have been wonderful,' said Robert.

'Not everyone thought so,' the young minister admitted. 'Some thought it was all emotion and not God's blessing at all. And many non-Christians were quite unaffected.'

'Will you go on with your story?' McCheyne asked.

Burns nodded. 'As I couldn't keep up with all the people who wanted to speak to a minister I called on others to help. Sometimes the church was far too small for all who wanted to hear the preaching and we had to meet in the churchyard too. Then the blessing spread beyond St Peter's to other churches. It seemed as if it would never stop.'

'And has it?'

Shaking his head, William explained that remarkable things were still happening in Dundee.

'I've prayed for God to send revival ever since I came to St Peter's,' Robert told one of his elders a few days later. 'And he answered my prayers when I wasn't even here.'

The elder, a shrewd and understanding man, looked his minister in the eye. 'How does that feel?' he asked.

McCheyne thought for a moment. 'If you're wondering if I'm feeling envious of the blessings God sent through William Burns's ministry here, the answer is that I'm not, not at all. I'm just so grateful for what has happened.'

And as time passed Robert discovered that many of those

who had been most affected by the revival had first been made to think through his preaching before he went off on his travels.

When McCheyne heard that several children's meetings were being held he was very pleased indeed. He was in the process of finding out more about them when there was a knock on his study door. Opening it he discovered two boys waiting to see him. Their names were Tom Brown and John Smith. They had brought a letter telling the minister about their prayer meeting. But as they were taken right to his study they were able to tell him face to face.

'I live in Small's Wynd Orphanage,' Tom explained, 'and we hold a children's prayer meeting in Isles Lane.'

'We used to hold it outside,' added John. 'But now we have the use of a room.'

'How many come to the meeting?' enquired McCheyne.

Tom held the letter open and the minister counted the children's signatures. There were 30 names in all, 18 boys and 12 girls.

'How old are the children who attend?' the boys were asked.

John explained that they were all 14 or younger.

'And how often do you meet?'

'We meet every evening, sir,' Tom said, 'at 6 o'clock.'

Robert tried to imagine thirty children crammed into a little room in the winter cold.

'What do you pray for?' he asked John.

'We pray for you and for Mr Burns,' the lad answered.

Putting his arms round the boys' shoulders, McCheyne thanked them and told them that their prayers were being answered.

On 31st December 1839 a number of young people

became members of St Peter's. Some of them attended the children's prayer meetings. Two of those who said publicly that Jesus was their Saviour were 10 years old, four were 14, and three were 15 or 16.

By summer the following year the revival was passing. Many had come to faith and were continuing in their love and service for the Lord. And many Christians who had been deeply challenged continued to grow in the faith. But those who had just been carried along on a tide of emotion went back to where they were before. Robert was kept very busy teaching those who had been converted during the revival and counselling others who were threatening to fall away. He also resumed visiting the area round the church. Once again his maps were on his study table and the names of those he visited were added each day when he returned home. The number of meetings held in the church increased, as did the size of congregation attending them.

McCheyne continued his contact with the children, especially any in need. One was a poor lad called Jamie Laing who lived in Miller's Wynd, not far from St Peter's. The lad was unwell and the minister went to visit him.

'What age are you?' Robert asked.

'I'm nearly 12,' said Jamie. And then he began to talk about himself. 'Mum died when I was seven and my sister looks after my brother and me. My brother held a prayer meeting in our home during the revival. But it was after that, during a prayer service, that I knew I wanted to become a Christian like my brother and sister. I suppose they'd been praying for me.'

McCheyne said he was sure that they had.

During the weeks that followed Robert visited that home often and Jamie's face lit up every time he arrived. It lit up even more when his minister spoke to him about Jesus. Jamie was in a great deal of pain. Once, when his Sunday School classmates visited him, the boy told them how he had been converted, and warned that they had to become Christians too or they'd not go to heaven when they died. But Jamie wasn't perfect and from time to time he confided in his minister about the temptations that troubled him. His illness progressed and he spent most of his time in bed. When McCheyne wrote this poem he may have had Jamie in mind.

> *Gentle Shepherd, on thy shoulder*
> *Carry me, a sinful lamb,*
> *Give me faith, and make me bolder,*
> *Till with thee in heaven I am.*

Robert was Jamie's friend through the last two years of his life. And when the boy died in June 1842 and went home to heaven his minister and friend conducted his funeral.

Although McCheyne was a faithful minister to the people of St Peter's he was not always to be found in Dundee. He travelled long distances to preach despite his health becoming increasingly precarious. Congregations in many parts of Scotland heard him speaking as did others in Ireland and England. And church politics also took up his time. The 1830s and early 1840s were troubled times in Scotland. Many members of the Church of Scotland, of which McCheyne was a minister, were becoming increasingly concerned that the government and landowners were interfering in church life. Congregations that ought to have been allowed to choose their own ministers were having men foisted upon them that they didn't want at all. Meeting after meeting was held about it, and Robert Murray McCheyne was deeply involved. He was one of the men who could see that a split was coming, that those who believed that congregations should be free to choose their own ministers would have to leave the Church of Scotland and set up the Free Church of Scotland, a church that would be free from political interference. The thought of a split saddened him though it didn't happen till two months after his death. His time was also taken up in helping Andrew Bonar write an account of the trip to investigate the possibility of missionary work among Jewish people. Because neither Robert nor Andrew Bonar had peace to write they exchanged homes and congregations for a month to concentrate on the job! Andrew had only to write the report while Robert was also responsible for the drawings that were in it.

The heavy workload McCheyne carried began to tell on his health again. But that didn't stop him going with some friends to Newcastle to take services there. One open-air meeting he spoke at was attended by around 1000 people!

'I'm going to travel home by Ruthwell and Clarencefield,' Robert wrote to Eliza. 'It's ages since I was there and I'd love to see the place again.'

When Robert arrived he discovered that three cousins were also visiting.

'Here's Mr Perfection!' Mary told her sisters, Charlotte and Georgiana. 'There won't be any fun this evening.'

'He's not too bad,' Charlotte thought.

'This is going to be hard going,' decided Georgiana.

'He's SO religious,' muttered Mary. 'Imagine having to spend days with him!'

Although the first evening may have dragged for the three young women, by the next morning they had come to respect their cousin. He really seemed to care about them. Before long Robert was telling them what Jesus meant to him. And by the time he left he had seen Mary, Charlotte and Georgiana become Christians. As the young man left on the journey home he was filled with joy at what had taken place.

McCheyne was not long home when he was invited to take Communion services in London at the end of November 1842. His health was poor and his elders in St Peter's were far from happy about him going away in the middle of winter. But when their minister said that he was sure it was God's will for him to go, they didn't force the issue. By the time he returned home again he was paler than ever and his cough was very troublesome.

'Would you like to come for a walk along the Tay?' he asked a friend, one sunny day that December.

'That would be good,' his friend agreed.

The two young men walked downhill to the Magdalen Yards and turned up-river when they came to the Tay.

'I don't think we should go as far as Perth,' teased Robert. 'I don't feel fit for a 23 mile hike!'

'Agreed,' said his friend, 'though I'm glad that William Burns went on to Perth from Dundee. God blessed his preaching and sent revival there too.'

'One of my elders asked me if I minded revival coming when I was away,' McCheyne remembered. 'But I was just thrilled that it happened at all.'

'You're so good,' the other young man said. 'I think I might have been a little jealous.'

Robert stopped and swung round. 'So good!' he said. 'If you could see the inside of my heart you'd know I'm not good. I have so many faults that only I know about, apart from those that other people see and hear. If I die young,' he went on, thinking of his failing health, 'the last thing I want is for people to remember me for what I was not. I'm a sinner saved by grace, and any good I've been able to say or do has been said or done by the grace of God, not because of anything special in Robert Murray McCheyne.'

They turned and walked back towards Dundee in silence. Robert's mind was on the gulls that wheeled overhead. His friend was wondering whether the young minister at his side would live long. He seemed to be getting paler and thinner with every month that passed.

'My friends,' McCheyne said, during the service on 30th December 1842, 'I have prepared a Scripture Calendar for you.'

The congregation listened with interest.

'I've divided the whole of the Bible into 365 sections, one for each day of the year. If you follow the Scripture Calendar and read the passages for each day you'll read the whole Bible in a year. And if you follow it year after year you'll grow to know it well.'

Many in the congregation took up the challenge and McCheyne's Bible reading scheme is still used today. With that he ended 1842, and the New Year began with Communion in St Peter's.

'February is not the best time to travel to

121

Aberdeenshire,' Eliza said, when she heard where her brother planned to go. 'It's even colder there than here.'

'You're a real nursemaid!' Robert teased. 'Don't you remember the fun we had in the snow when we were children?'

Eliza laughed. 'I certainly do! And I remember you throwing snowballs in my direction too!'

But it was not snowballs that nearly hit Robert as he preached north of Aberdeen. Several people took up handfuls of stones to pelt him. But as soon as he began to speak their hands fell to their sides and the stones slipped down to the ground.

'Today the snow is beginning to drift,' he wrote a day or two later. 'But God is with us and he'll look after us. I'm fine apart from feeling a bit tired sometimes.'

On 1st March McCheyne arrived back in Dundee, but there was no Eliza to look after him as she was spending some time back home in Edinburgh. Robert wrote to his sister telling her about his trip north.

'I'm truly happy to be home from my wanderings. I preached and spoke 27 times in 24 different places.'

But things were not good in Dundee. Typhoid fever struck the area round the church and people were ill and dying from it. Robert went from house to house visiting people who were sick with fever. Tired though he was he went on with the work.

'They might die without knowing their need of Jesus,' he told himself, as he hoisted his tired body out of the chair and reached for his coat. 'I must tell them before it's too late.'

McCheyne preached three times on Sunday 12th March

1843, and on Monday attended a meeting about the problems in the Church of Scotland. But having spoken earnestly at the meeting he arrived home exhausted, shivery and sick. Unwell though he was, the following day he took a wedding.

'Will 'oo put this in 'oor coat?' a small girl asked the minister as she handed him a flower.

'O yes, my dear,' he said, helping the child to pin it on.

'Now I have done what you wanted will you do what I want?' he asked.

The girl said she would.

'Well,' said Robert, 'I would like you to listen to the story of the Good Shepherd who gave his life for his sheep.'

Five or six other children gathered around and he told them about Jesus.

By the time McCheyne arrived home it was clear that he was suffering from fever. When news of his illness spread it was as if the west end of Dundee came to a standstill.

'Have you heard how he is?' people enquired when they met.

Nobody needed to ask who 'he' was. The 29-year-old minister was in everyone's mind. Christians met in churches and homes to pray for him and their prayers were answered, though not in the way many hoped. On 25th March, instead of making Robert well God did something much better, because he took him home to heaven where he would never again be ill or in pain, where he would never again weep or mourn.

But the people of Dundee mourned the loss of the man they loved, and others in Scotland and beyond were also sad at the news. After Robert died a letter arrived at his home that had been posted before news of his illness reached the writer. It was from someone who had heard him preach his last sermon. The letter read, 'I saw in you a beauty in holiness that I never saw before.' The amazing truth is that before the letter arrived Robert Murray McCheyne was as beautiful in holiness as the Lord Jesus Christ, because God has promised that those whose sins are forgiven will be like Jesus when they die. So it was that as one life of adventure ended there began the most glorious adventure of all.

Thinking Further Topics

Chapter 1
A Good Game of Squirrels

Robert enjoyed spending time with friends, and kept in touch with some all of his life. How important is friendship to you? Jesus had twelve disciples. Were any of them special friends (John 20:2, John 21:7)? How do we maintain special friendships without being exclusive and making others feel unwelcome?

Robert went on holiday to Dumfriesshire regularly. He enjoyed the countryside. When he was on holiday he attended church in Ruthwell. Do you make a point of going to church when on holiday, or do you take a holiday from church too? Does God ever have a holiday from caring for us (Psalm 121:3-4, 7-8)?

When Robert was a boy there were no computers or Playstations. Do you think that young people then were bored because they had no high-tech toys? What are your simple pleasures? What hobbies and pastimes could you enjoy if there was a day-long electricity strike and no batteries left in the shops?

Chapter 2
Winter Sets In

Robert was aware of the beauty of creation. He lived before Darwin's Theory of Evolution was formulated. What would Robert have believed about the beginning of all things (Genesis 1)? Should we believe men's theories when they contradict God's word?

Family life was important to the McCheynes. Is your family important to you? Whose idea was family life (Genesis 2:22)? The McCheynes spent time together. Do you spend time with your family, or are you so glued to the television or a book (even a Christian book!) that you hardly notice other people?

David McCheyne showed his respect for his father by writing a poem for him on his birthdays. What does the Bible say about respecting parents (Exodus 20:12)? Paul says this too (Ephesians 6:1-3) but what does he say to fathers (Ephesians 6:4)?

Chapter 3
The Great Fire of Edinburgh

The steeple of the Tron Church in Edinburgh collapsed in the fire, and at first it looked as though the church was devastated. Is the church a building? Or is the church the people who worship in it? The Bible calls Jesus the 'living Stone'. Are you a living stone in the living church (1 Peter 2:4-6)?

Robert McCheyne was the same age as the young lad he met outside the Tron Church. They lived in the same city, but they came from opposite ends of the social scale. The boy was poor and uneducated while Robert was the opposite. Do you react differently to rich and poor people (James 2:1-5)? The Bible tells us that the Lord became poor in order to save his people (2 Corinthians 8:9).

David tried to explain to Robert what a Christian is. How would you define a Christian? God explained to Nicodemus what it meant to be a Christian in John 3:16-18.

Chapter 4
David

David McCheyne's example made a life-changing impression on his young brother. If you are a Christian, do your family members see a difference in your life? The Bible tells us what that difference should be (1 John 2:9-11). But however long we live we are never perfect in this life. John has good news for us when we disgrace the Christian faith by how we behave (1 John 1:8-9).

When David was seriously ill Robert prayed that he would recover. But God's will was to take David home to heaven. In Gethsemane Jesus prayed that if it were possible he should not have to die on the cross. But what did he go on to pray (Mark 14:36)? When you have a worry or concern, can you ask for God's will to be done rather than your own? It's not easy, but it is the example Christ has given us.

None of the notes or letters that remain from Robert Murray

McCheyne give a date or exact account of his conversion. Paul could give the date, time and place of his conversion experience (Acts 9:1-19). Was Paul somehow superior to Robert because of this? The important thing is not the time and place of conversion, but the fact of it. Some very prominent Christians are unable to say exactly when they came to faith.

Chapter 5
Travels with Tully

When an old Christian man died Robert was able to comfort his relatives. Why was that (John 3:16)? That fact that believers have eternal life and go to heaven when they die is a comfort. Does that mean we shouldn't feel sad when someone dies, even if that person is a Christian? How did Jesus feel when his friend Lazarus died (John 11:35)? If you are sad because you've lost someone you love Jesus remembers and understands how you feel.

Robert's memories of David were precious to him but he also looked forward to seeing him again in heaven. Do you ever think about heaven? Read Revelation 7:9-17. What will there not be in heaven (v 16)? Who will be in heaven (vs 9 and 14)? Read how tenderly the Lord will deal with those who go to heaven (v 17). Heaven really is somewhere to look forward to.

The young man in Larbert must have been surprised when he received Robert's letter and discovered that his minister understood him. Do you think of your minister as being so different that he can't possibly understand what it's like to be young? Remember your minister was young once himself. Perhaps he would tell you about his youth if you asked him.

Chapter 6
Rescued from a Tree

From boyhood Robert was keen on gymnastics, and we know from accounts written about him that he was very good. Gymnasts improve with training. The Bible has something to say about going into training (1 Timothy 4:8). How can you train yourself to be godly (1 Timothy 4:7)? God has given us some apparatus: prayer, the Bible, Christian friends, church.

Robert had a reputation of being good with children and young people. He valued them for themselves. In this he was following Jesus' example (Mark 10:13-16). Do you feel valued by believers? Do you value those younger than yourself?

When Robert went to Dundee he was ordained as a minister of the gospel. Timothy was a minister. What charge did Paul give him (2 Timothy 4:1-4)? Both Timothy and Robert were young men. What did Paul say about being a youthful pastor (1 Timothy 4:12)? In order to show maturity, in what areas of life does a young person have to be an example?

Chapter 7
'Hey Minister!'

Not all churches were full in Robert McCheyne's day, but many were. Is your church full? Does it affect your worship if your church is half empty? Who is the focus of your worship (Psalm 95:6-7)? What does Jesus say about small numbers (Matthew 18:20)? Although it may be easier to feel the presence of God among a crowd of worshippers, he is there where only two or three are gathered.

Robert was asked if he would move from Dundee to Skirling, where the climate and workload would have been better suited to his health. But he believed he was where God wanted him to be. How do we know God's will for our lives? Does the Bible give detailed guidance or general principles that we have to apply to find God's will? Some of the principles are found in the Ten Commandments (Exodus 20:1-17) and in Psalm 37 and Proverbs 3:1-7:27.

Prayer meetings were very much a feature of the life of St Peter's Church. Does your church have a prayer meeting? Do you attend it? It has been said that the prayer meeting is the powerhouse of a congregation. If your church doesn't have a prayer meeting, perhaps you could meet with a friend to pray for your minister and congregation.

Chapter 8
Crash Landing!

Robert wrote an amusing poem to his doctor. Do you feel that Christians have to be so serious that they can't have any fun? Or do you feel the opposite, that life is too much fun to consider being seriously committed to the Lord? Who gave us the gift of humour? Philippians 4:8-9 tells us what Christians should think about, and there are many truly funny situations, jokes, books, films and programmes that fit into God's guidelines. He doesn't ask us to be kill-joys, just to be careful.

The Jews were God's chosen people in Old Testament times. Many times God calls them 'my people'. See Psalm 81:8, Isaiah 40:1. Now Christians are God's special chosen people. See 2 Corinthians 6:16. God promised Abraham that he would have a son. Isaac was the fulfilment of that promise. God also promised Abraham that he would have as many descendants are there are stars in the sky (Genesis 15:5). Who are these descendants (Galatians 4:28)?

Although the Jewish people rejected the Lord Jesus, how do we know that they are still to be told the good news that he is their promised Messiah (Luke 24:47)? Where was the gospel to be preached first, before it was taken to all nations?

Chapter 9
Journey of Discovery

Many Jewish people live in Palestine, which is one of the most troubled parts of the world. What does God ask us to do (Psalm 122:6-7)? Do you pray for the trouble spots of the world when you hear about them on the news? Are you so used to hearing about fighting and wars that you don't actually take in that real people are involved?

Anti-Semitism is a terrible evil. The history of World War 2 gives shameful examples of anti-Semitism. Do you know any Jewish people? Do you have among your friends people from other countries and cultures?

Robert McCheyne and Andrew Bonar visited a school just as a child was being physically punished. Today physical punishment is frowned upon, even outlawed in some countries. What does the Bible say about the subject (Proverbs 13:24)? Is there a difference between controlled physical punishment and violence against a child?

Chapter 10
An End and a New Beginning

It must be wonderful to live at a time of revival, when great crowds of people come to know the Lord. From whom does revival come (Habakkuk 3:2)? What happens when revival comes (Habakkuk 3:3-7)? The prophet couldn't organise a revival but what was he able to do (Habakkuk 3:1)? Might you pray for revival in your heart, your church and your country?

Robert prepared a Bible reading scheme for his people to follow. The Bible is God's living word. How else is it described (Ephesians 6:17)? A sword is used both as a weapon and for defence. How can you use the Bible as a weapon and for your defence (Matthew 4:1-11)? Perhaps you could use a reading scheme like the one McCheyne drew up.

What does the Bible say will happen when the Lord comes again (1 John 3:2)? Christians who die and go to heaven before the Lord's Second Coming will also be transformed into the image of Jesus. Our minds simply can't take that in. Use some of the heavenly songs from the book of Revelation to praise God for the glory that is to come (Revelation 5:12-13, 7:10-12, 19:5-8).

Robert Murray McCheyne Timeline

1807	Highland Clearances begin. Many Scottish people emigrate to America, Australia, Canada.
	Abolition of the Slave trade in the U.K.
1809	Louis Braille born.
1812	Charles Dickens born.
1813	Robert Murray McCheyne born.
	Jane Austin's 'Pride and Prejudice' published.
1814	Francis Scott Key wrote "The Star Spangled Banner."
	The first steam locomotive invented by George Stephenson.
	First photograph taken by Joseph Nicéphone Niépce.
1815	The Battle of Waterloo and the defeat of Napoleon.
1819	Stethoscope invented by René Laënnec.
1822	Caledonian Canal opened.
1824	George MacDonald, novelist, born.
1827	Robert Murray McCheyne enters university.

1829	Typewriter invented by W. A. Burt.
1831	Robert Murray McCheyne begins his theological education.
	Robert Murray McCheyne's conversion.
	Faraday discovers electro-magnetic induction.
1833	Emancipation of Slaves in the U.K.
	Factory Act forbids employment of children below the age of 9.
1835	Continuous Electric light invented by James Bowman Lindsay.
1837	Queen Victoria ascends the throne.
1839	The bicycle is invented.
1841	Stapler invented by Samuel Slocum.
1843	Robert Murray McCheyne dies.
	Disruption of the Church of Scotland.
	Charles Dickens publishes 'A Christmas Carol.'
	Foundation of the Free Church of Scotland.
1845	Pneumatic tyre invented by Robert Thomson.
1846	Anaesthesia developed by James Young Simpson.
1847	Antiseptics invented by Ignaz Semmelweis.

Robert Murray McCheyne
Life Summary

Robert was born in 1813 into a legal family in Edinburgh, Scotland's capital city. A short walk from their home would take Robert to the city centre and a view of its famous castle. After attending the High School Robert went to Edinburgh University. His subjects included Greek, Latin, French, gymnastics and elocution. He also wrote poetry, both in English, Latin and Greek!

Despite having been brought up in a church going home, Robert did not come to a personal faith in Jesus as a child. He thought that living a good life was what Christianity was all about. When his brother David was a young man he developed tuberculosis. Robert, who loved his brother dearly, was greatly impressed by the peace and joy with which he died in 1831. It was as a result of being with David at his death that Robert came to a personal faith in the Lord Jesus Christ, something he wrote about over and again. By then Robert was a student for the ministry of the Church of Scotland.

In 1835 Robert became assistant minister to Rev John Bonar in Larbert and Dunipace. The following year he went to Dundee to be ordained as minister of St Peter's Church. This was in a poor area of the city where disease was rife. It was not the best place for someone with delicate health, but Robert knew that was where God wanted him to be. His sister Eliza kept house for him.

Robert was not long in Dundee before his church began to fill. He was one of the most gifted preachers of his day and people came from great distances to listen to him. His preaching especially moved young people, and many became Christians under his ministry. However, their minister was plagued with ill health, and towards the end of 1838 he was advised to take a lengthy period off work. He went home to his parents in Edinburgh to rest and recover.

At that time the Church of Scotland was interested in reaching out to Jewish people with the gospel. It was arranged to send a fact-finding delegation to Jerusalem and other parts of Europe where there were Jewish communities. One of the delegation had to pull out for health reasons, and Robert – whose health was far from good – was invited to go instead. Always interested in missions, and especially interested in the Jewish people, he accepted the invitation. Along with Andrew Bonar, Alexander Keith and Alexander Black, Robert spent several months abroad.

Just before they returned to Scotland, Andrew Bonar and Robert heard news of a revival in Dundee, but it was not until they were back home that they discovered that the locum minister, whom Robert had left in charge, had been at the centre of the revival. Wonderful things had happened in McCheyne's absence, things he had prayed for ever since becoming minister of St Peters. Delighted at the revival, and thrilled at the conversions that had taken place and the sleepy Christians whose faith had been enlivened, Robert again took over as minister of St Peters.

The 1840s were difficult in Scottish church history, and Robert was very involved in efforts to prevent the State trying to interfere with the church. This came to a head in May 1843 when the Free Church of Scotland was formed. But just a few weeks before that happened God took Robert home to heaven after yet another illness. His death hit Dundee hard. Windows were darkened and businesses closed as a mark of respect for the 29 year old minister who had died. Although Robert Murray McCheyne was ordained for less than seven years, he was one of the most influential ministers in the 19th Century, and his memory is still highly regarded both in Scotland and abroad.

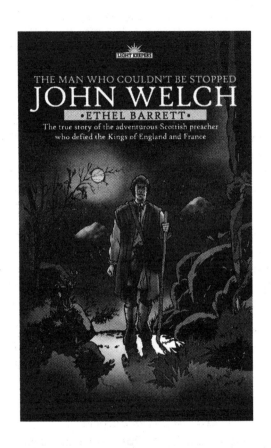

THE MAN WHO COULDN'T BE STOPPED
JOHN WELCH
·ETHEL BARRETT·

The true story of the adventurous Scottish preacher
who defied the Kings of England and France

New Lightkeepers Material!
JOHN WELCH

John Welch just couldn't be stopped.

When he was a boy he was independent, stubborn and had a mind of his own. It all ended in tears as he ran away from his father, fell in with a gang of thieves and began a life of stealing and robbery. It seemed as though he had chosen his life and nothing and no one could stop him. But then he met God. John left his sinful life and became a preacher and with God beside him there was nothing and no one who could stand in his way – not even the King of England or the King of France! This is the true story of one of Scotland's most adventurous preachers.

As the son-in-law of another fiery Scot – John Knox – John Welch was bound to cause a stir – and he did! Find out about how he conquered roughians, saved a town from the dreaded plague and even dodged a cannon ball!

Extra Features include:
Maps, Quiz, Time Line, What was life like then?
And Fact Summaries

ISBN :1-85792-928-4

Torchbearers
Danger On The Hill
by C. Mackenzie

"Run, run for your lives," a young boy screamed. "Run, everybody, run. The soldiers are here."

That day on the hill is the beginning of a new and terrifying life for the three Wilson children. Margaret, Agnes and Thomas are not afraid to stand up for what they believe in, but it means that they are forced to leave their home and their parents for a life of hiding on the hills.

If you were a covenanter in the 1600s you were the enemy of the King and the authorities. But all you really wanted to do was worship God in the way he told you to in the Bible. Margaret wants to give Jesus Christ the most important place in her life, and this conviction might cost her life. **There is danger on the hill for Margaret. There is danger everywhere - if you are a covenanter. The** Torchbearers series are true life stories from history where Christians have suffered and died for their faith in Christ.

ISBN I 85792 7842

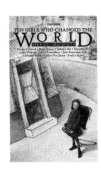  

Start collecting this series now!

Ten Girls who changed the World
Corrie Ten Boom, Mary Slessor,
Joni Eareckson Tada, Isobel Kuhn,
Amy Carmichael, Elizabeth Fry, Evelyn Brand,
Gladys Aylward, Catherine Booth,
Jackie Pullinger

Ten Girls who made a Difference
Monica of Thagaste,
Catherine Luther, Susanna Wesley,
Ann Judson, Maria Taylor,
Susannah Spurgeon, Bethan Lloyd-Jones,
Edith Schaeffer, Sabina Wurmbrand,
Ruth Bell Graham.

Ten Girls who made History
Ida Scudder, Betty Green, Jeanette Li,
Mary Jane Kinnaird, Bessie Adams,
Emma Dryer, Lottie Moon,
Florence Nightingale,
Heanrietta Mears, Elisabeth Elliot.

Start collecting this series now!

Ten Boys who changed the World
David Livingstone, Billy Graham,
Brother Andrew, John Newton, William Carey,
George Müller, Nicky Cruz,
Eric Liddell, Luis Palau, Adoniram Judson.

Ten Boys who made a Difference
Augustine of Hippo,
Jan Hus, Martin Luther,
Ulrich Zwingli, William Tyndale,
Hugh Latimer, John Calvin,
John Knox, Lord Shaftesbury,
Thomas Chalmers.

Ten Boys who made History
Charles Spurgeon, Jonathan Edwards,
Samuel Rutherford, D L Moody,
Martin Lloyd Jones, A. W. Tozer, John Owen,
Robert Murray McCheyne, Billy Sunday,
George Whitefield.

Heroes to look up to!
The Trailblazer Series

Trailblazers

Corrie ten Boom, The Watchmaker's Daughter
ISBN 1 85792 116X
Joni Eareckson Tada, Swimming against the Tide
ISBN 1 85792 833 4
Adoniram Judson, Danger on the Streets of Gold
ISBN 1 85792 6609
Isobel Kuhn, Lights in Lisuland
ISBN 1 85792 6102
C.S. Lewis, The Story Teller
ISBN 1 85792 4878
Martyn Lloyd-Jones, From Wales to Westminster
ISBN 1 85792 3499
George Müller, The Children's Champion
ISBN 1 85792 5491
John Newton, A Slave Set Free NEW
ISBN 1 85792 834 2
John Paton, A South Sea Island Rescue
ISBN 1 85792 852 0
Mary Slessor, Servant to the Slave
ISBN 1 85792 3480
Hudson Taylor, An Adventure Begins
ISBN 1 85792 4231
William Wilberforce, The Freedom Fighter
ISBN 1 85792 3715
Richard Wurmbrand, A Voice in the Dark
ISBN 1 85792 2980
Gladys Aylward, No Mountain Too High
ISBN 1 85792 5947

CHRISTIAN FOCUS

Staying faithful - Reaching out!

Christian Focus Publications publishes books for adults and children under its three main imprints: Christian Focus, Mentor and Christian Heritage. Our books reflect that God's word is reliable and Jesus is the way to know him, and live for ever with him.

Our children's publication list includes a Sunday school curriculum that covers pre-school to early teens; puzzle and activity books. We also publish personal and family devotional titles, biographies and inspirational stories that children will love.

If you are looking for quality Bible teaching for children then we have an excellent range of Bible story and age specific theological books.

From pre-school to teenage fiction, we have it covered!

Find us at our web page:
www.christianfocus.com